British History

An Illustrated Guide

Hugh Williams

St Edward's Press Ltd

Formal Notes

British History – An Illustrated Guide

First published in 2016 by
St Edward's Press Ltd

1st edition

ISBN 978-0- 9554188-6-0

Further copies of this book may be ordered by emailing the publishers at info@stedwardspress.co.uk or via post to Hugh Williams, 20 Barra Close, Highworth, Wilts, SN67HX..

Cover Design by Stables Creative Design, Highworth

Printed by Ashford Colour Press Ltd

British History – An illustrated Guide

Contents

Dedication

For Andrew, Catherine, Lucy, Nicholas, Francesca, Luke and Robert.

Acknowledgements

I must thank my wife, Alice, for, possibly inadvertently, giving me the idea of writing this book. She also needs thanking for her patience during all the hours that I have buried myself away putting this book together.

I am also very grateful to my daughter, Martha Williams, for her wisdom and help with the design, and also to those who have allowed me to use their images, many without charge. In fact their willingness to help, and the enthusiasm with which so many people have encouraged the preparation of this work, have been of far more assistance towards this project than they may have realised.

Mention must of course be made that this book could not have been prepared without the camera given to me by all my friends in my old office, now H M Williams Chartered Certified Accountants, in Plympton. Knowing that I needed a camera for this project, they all kindly clubbed together and bought it for me as a retirement present. I carry it with me wherever I go.

I am also hugely indebted to Daniel Joyce for his patient, untiring and invaluable help with editing this work and also to many other kind people who have reviewed this book before publication and have suggested improvements and corrections. All of which means that any errors are clearly down to the author!

Where no attribution has been given alongside a photograph it is because it was taken by the author.

Hugh Williams
2016

Introduction and to set the scene…

Bill Bryson has kindly given permission to set the scene in the following way:

Bill Bryson said the following of Britain (BBC 4 Ramblings 26th September 2015):"In this tiny island, wherever you go, historical stuff is just packed in". He was describing the setting in which he found himself, standing with Clare Balding on the Long Walk in Windsor Great Park.

The Long Walk leading to Windsor Castle.
© Chrislophotos / Shutterstock.com

Within a mile or so of where he was standing, he mentioned that he was close to all of these places and more:

- Frogmore Mausoleum, where Queen Victoria is buried. She died in 1901.

- The village of Horton, where John Milton wrote *Paradise Lost* (first published in 1667).

- The Memorial at Runnymede to mark the place where King John signed Magna Carta (1215).

- The Air Forces Memorial (unveiled by H M Queen Elizabeth II in 1953).

- Eton College (founded in 1440 by King Henry VI) with its copy of the Guttenberg Bible (first printed in 1455).

School Yard at Eton © Basphoto / Shutterstock.com

And, of course…

- Windsor Castle with all of *its* history (the original castle was built in 11th Century, after the Norman invasion) .

Windsor Castle from the River Thames © Basphoto / Shutterstock.com

He then went on to say, "If I parachuted you just randomly into a place in (say) the Midlands, you would be within five miles of something that is globally important and really significant. It's amazing that so much has happened here in such a small area."

In other words (and assuming you are either already in Britain, or planning to visit the island) we join Bill Bryson in hoping that you will be astonished at just how much "historical stuff" there is to be seen and experienced here.

To support what Bill Bryson has said, and to help you understand British history, we have laid out this book in nine easy steps with a tenth step being the appendices.

When you use the index, please note that items in the index are located by their reference date and not by page number. Reference dates should be easily found on each page and, to help you track down a date, the beginning and end dates of the relevant step are always shown at the top of each page.

We hope that this book will help you discover historical information that entertains and enlightens you, and, above all, tells you more about British history than you knew before.

Step 1. Before the Coming of the Romans (4,000BC to 55BC)

Introduction

We tend to be taught that British History began with the coming of the Romans – and indeed that they were the first bringers of civilisation to these islands. However, and as those who study Celtic history will tell you, the Romans, like the members of any usurping empire (or would-be empire) were not popular; they dealt ruthlessly with the people they found there and, being the victors, left them with a history that suppresses what happened before they arrived. This is why we all tend to know so little about pre-Roman Britain. To address this problem, we start with the three well-known "ages", Stone, Bronze and Iron.

Before we start we need to stress that there are significant difficulties using terms like Stone Age because (1) they are only general terms, (2) archaeologists tend to disagree about their relevance and how long they lasted and (3) the period that they are assumed to have lasted in one geographical area may not cover the same length of time that it covered in another. Nonetheless the terms are in common usage and so it should be helpful if we start with them.

4,000 BC to 2,500 BC Stone Age Britain

If we take the earliest period, the Stone Age, about which very little is known, the people who inhabited Britain tended to live in caves such as Kent's Cavern in Torquay.

Kent's Cavern, Torquay.Photo by kind permission of Kent's Cavern Ltd©

And they used flints which they mined at places such as Grimes Graves in Norfolk.

2,500BC to c1,500BC Bronze Age Britain

While we may not know very much about Stone Age Britain our island's history is far from void when it comes to the Bronze Age. The inhabitants of Bronze Age Britain used implements made of, unsurprisingly, bronze (an alloy of copper and tin). The use of bronze is thought to have been introduced to this country by the Beaker Folk who had arrived from the continent to settle in Britain. These peoples also developed an early form of writing known as proto-writing. There are plenty of sites connected to the Bronze Age that can be visited, probably the most famous of which being Stonehenge, which we will come to shortly, and similar ancient structures.

The Celts

Excluding those who lived during the Stone Age, it was the Celts who first occupied the island of Britain. Whilst few historians agree on dates, there is a general consensus that there was a migration of people in a north-westerly direction across the continent of Europe during the second millennium BC. Those who settled in the British Isles, as we say, were Celts. These were the people who built or erected the great Bronze Age structures like Stonehenge and the associated hut settlements and barrows.

Stonehenge near Amesbury in Wiltshire

And it was the Celts who erected structures like these standing stones at Callanish on the Isle of Lewis in the Outer Hebrides, Scotland

Standing stones at Callanish
© Bieler Michael / Shutterstock.com

… And also the White Horse at Uffington in Oxfordshire,

The Uffington White Horse – the oldest in Britain and dating back to the Bronze Age

or the fascinating things you can see in the village of Avebury in Wiltshire.

Scenes at Avebury: The man-made Silbury Hill and some of the many standing stones in the village

Who were the Celts?

Christian tradition holds that it was the Celts who were the original inhabitants of Europe after the dispersal of peoples from Mesopotamia (in Iraq) following the collapse of the Tower of Babel. Even today, long since the Celts were driven back to the North West fringes of Europe by the Romans and others, there is a remarkably distinctive and consistent DNA sequence to be found in the peoples who live in these areas, particularly in Cornwall, Wales, the Isle of Man, Galloway and the Hebrides.

Celtic Language and Religion

Some even say that their language, Gaelic, was the language spoken in the Garden of Eden, which is believed to have been in Mesopotamia. This may be fanciful, but there are at least two indications that this may be true:

- Indian Sanskrit contains many words that are similar to Gaelic, and, to some ears, there is a distinct similarity between the actual sounds of the Welsh and Indian dialects. In other words, the contention goes, might this not suggest that both have the same origin in Mesopotamia, which lies roughly halfway between where these two peoples now live?
- There is a tradition in the Basque Country (on the north coast of Spain) that the language they speak is the same language as Noah and that it was brought to their land by Tubal, Noah's grandson.

The religion of the Celts at this time was usually Druidism. However, it would be from their number that Christian missionaries such as St Patrick and St Columba would spread Christianity through Northern Europe.

13th C BC The first recorded event in British History?

While this is the subject of speculation, and even dismissal, there are those who hold that the first event that has been recorded in British History was the arrival of Brutus from Troy in the thirteenth century BC (please note that he is not the same Brutus that we associate with Julius Caesar). He was the grandson of Aeneas, a cousin of the Trojan King, and he escaped from Troy after the Greeks had destroyed it. At that stage, the island of Britain was known as Albion, but Brutus changed the name to Britannicus. According to Geoffrey of Monmouth, he landed at Totnes, but he founded and made his capital city London, which he called Trinovantum (New Troy).

The Brutus Stone at Totnes and the banks of the River Dart, where it flows through Totnes.

Britain is divided into three countries and the British people start to be identified

Brutus divided the island between his sons Locrinus, Camber and Albanactus. Locrinus received (roughly) what we now call England, Camber was given Wales (hence Cambria, Cambrian Mountains, etc.) and Albanactus received the part that is now Scotland, which was then named after him and called Alba or Albany. Brutus's second-in-command was called Corineus, and, in reward for his services, Brutus gave him the land we now know as Cornwall. What this implies is that the British are part Celtic and part Trojan.

Humber

Shortly after Brutus's arrival, Humber, King of the Huns (a tribe of nomads who came from Eastern Europe), attacked Britain, but he was defeated. He drowned in the estuary that bears his name.

The Humber Estuary. © Electric Blue / Shutterstock.com

The Welsh

While on the subject of the British, it has been said that the only people who are still entitled to call themselves British are, in fact, the Welsh. This is because they still speak the same language of 3,000 years ago. Whereas, after the coming of the Saxons, the original native language in the rest of Britain disappeared; for example, in due course, English replaced Gaelic (the original language spoken in Scotland). The Gaelic language is however currently enjoying a significant resurgence in parts of Scotland.

The Scots

The confusing thing is that, at this stage, the people called Scots lived in Ireland which was then called Hibernia. The Scots may have got their name from one of their leaders having married an Egyptian princess called Scota. Accordingly, the people living in Alba (modern Scotland) were the British; they were not called Picts until the Romans invaded and called them Picts, because they wore paint. The Scots from Hibernia started colonising south west Alba soon after the Romans had departed from Britain and sometime after that the whole of Alba became known as Scotland.

C 1,500BC to 1st C AD   Iron Age

By this time we have reached the Iron Age where people worked in (again unsurprisingly) iron and even steel (an alloy of iron and carbon), which enabled them to improve their agricultural practices. They also developed religious beliefs and artistic styles, principally found today in ornaments and pottery. There are many Iron Age sites in Britain; one of the more famous is that of the remains of the hill fort, Old Sarum

Old Sarum, the remains of an Iron Age hill fort near Salisbury in Wiltshire.

One of the most characteristic signs of an Iron Age hill fort are marked defensive ramparts which can been seen in many parts of the country, such as at Wittenham in Oxfordshire:

Typical earthworks at an Iron Age hill fort. Wittenham Clumps, Oxfordshire.

And then there are the somewhat enigmatic Brochs, which are hollow-walled (probably defensive) structures found in Scotland.

The Broch of Mousa in Shetland. © TT Photos / Shutterstock.com

It would appear that one of the first towns in England was Abingdon, with evidence of it having existed from Iron Age times.

4th C BC Pytheas the Greek

Having just heard that the Iron Age inhabitants of Britain wore paint, the sailor and early explorer of the then known world, Pytheas the Greek, visited Britain in the 4th century BC, and according to one source, the name of Britain may arise from the word Pretannikai, or painted people. It would appear that that is how the Gauls, who lived in Armorica (northern France and particularly Brittany) described the people of Britain because they wore Woad (blue dye).

The Belgae

This was a tribe who lived in an area corresponding (very roughly) to modern Belgium. They settled in an area in southern Britain that covered (roughly) Dorset and Somerset.

The Kings of Britain

At this point, the much better-documented period of history is about to begin but, before we get going with that, you should be aware that there were apparently nearly 100 kings of Britain after Brutus. We do not plan to give all their names here, but what we will do is select a few names from the list with their rough dates because their existence may interest you.

1050BC	King Ebraucus, who gave his name to what we now know as York (Ebor).
1000BC	King Leil, who gave his name to Carlisle.

C 900BC	King Leir, who gave his name to Leicester, and on whose life Shakespeare based his famous play.
C 400BC	King Belinus, who gave his name to Billingsgate in London
55BC	Roman landings.
C 50BC	King Lud, who renamed Trinovantum, London, and gave his name to Ludgate in London.

And then, while on this subject of British kings, the following British kings reigned *after* the Romans invaded, and they, or their names, may be of interest:

43AD	King Cassivellaunus, who tried (ultimately) unsuccessfully to defend the country against the Roman invasion.
125AD	King Sulgenius. It was during his reign that the Romans built Hadrian's Wall.
3rd C AD	King Cole (or Coel) who founded Colchester and is believed to be the father of Helena, the mother of the Roman Emperor Constantine. Helena is a Saint in the Roman calendar and is believed to be responsible for locating the site of the crucifixion in Jerusalem and for recovering some very important Christian relics that can now be seen at, for example, the church of Santa Croce in Rome.
C 4th C AD	King Maximianus. He took control of what was then known as Armorica in northern France and renamed it Second Britain, hence we get the name of Brittany.
449AD	King Vortigern, who let in the Saxons.
C 6th C AD	King Arthur, about whom many famous legends have been invented. We have no way of knowing how much of his story is true, but he is reckoned to have been born in Tintagel in Cornwall and ruled not just Britain, but, in addition, Ireland, Scotland, Iceland, Norway, Denmark and most of the northern part of France. He is reputed to have been mortally wounded at the Battle of Slaughter Bridge in Cornwall. Please see photographs on the following page.

Tintagel Castle, Cornwall

Shortly after King Arthur we link up with King Egbert whose name appears at the top of the list of English Kings and Queens in the Appendix, where, in case you thought that we might have forgotten him, you will find mention of King Alfred the Great (a British king who reigned after the coming of the Saxons and Danes) about whom we say more later.

As has already been mentioned, most of this early history of Britain can be gleaned from the writings of Welshman Geoffrey of Monmouth, who is regarded in some, but by no means all, quarters as being "The Father of British History". He died about 1155AD.

Let us now move to where the facts are far more widely agreed upon, the Invasion by the Romans and what happened thereafter.

Step 2. From the Romans to the Norman Invasion (55BC to 1066)

55BC Roman Landings

The Romans first landed at Deal in Kent but they only stayed a few days. Their leader was Julius Caesar, who was assassinated in 44BC. Next year, 54BC, there was another short invasion.
At that time Britons wore paint called Woad.

1AD – 30AD Did Jesus Christ visit England?

What follows is highly likely to be pure legend because the Catholic Church has no tradition whatever of it being true. Nonetheless there is increasing interest in this idea and it might be helpful to give the following explanation of the meaning of the Hymn *Jerusalem*:

The legend goes that between 12 and 30AD we have no record of Christ's doings nor of His whereabouts. After the death of St Joseph, Jesus *may* have become the ward of St Joseph of Arimathea, His uncle. This Joseph was an importer of tin and other minerals. He is reckoned to have visited West Cornwall, the centre of the world's tin production and that he *might* have taken his ward with him. Local Cornish tradition states that they visited Ding Dong mine near Land's End and also stayed for some time near the lead mines in Somerset, near Glastonbury.

Ding Dong Mine, West Cornwall

This local tradition says that this supposed visit *may* explain why the Celtic Christian Church in West Cornwall was so strong and also why Glastonbury is considered by so many to be a deeply mystical place.

Glastonbury Tor, Somerset

One reason why Jesus, if he did indeed come to Britain, is thought to have chosen Glastonbury is because it was a strong centre of Druidism which, like Zoroastrianism, is a God-centred faith that looked for and depicted a Redeemer. Indeed there is evidence that St Joseph of Arimathea returned to Glastonbury within a few years of the Resurrection to look after the dwelling where he and Jesus had stayed, and to bring the Christian Faith to Glastonbury at a very early stage. There are some who maintain that he brought with him the Holy Grail, the Chalice that Christ used at the Last Supper and that this is the origin of the relic at Strata Florida, near Aberystwyth in Wales.

The remains of Glastonbury Abbey today

There is also a school of thought that, while in Britain, St Joseph of Arimathea built the very first Christian Church in the World, possibly / probably at Glastonbury. After all, neither Palestine nor Rome allowed Christians to worship Jesus, let alone build churches. To further support this view, the British bishops were held in high esteem at Catholic Councils in the early centuries – the reason given was, as we have just seen, that they represented the country that could claim to have built the first Christian Churches. (While mentioning

this, it is interesting to discover that, in Brittany, the French openly acknowledge that Christianity was brought to them from England.)
As is stressed, this tradition, that Christ visited England, can only be regarded as unsubstantiated legend, but, if it is true, it would explain why Christianity was already strongly established in South West Britain when St Augustine of Canterbury arrived in Kent in 596AD (see later). It would also explain why, if the French in Brittany acknowledge that it was the inhabitants of the South West of England who first brought Christianity to them, both areas share many places dedicated to Celtic Saints.
As already indicated, this may explain the words in William Blake's poem and hymn *Jerusalem,* when we sing "And did those Feet in ancient times, walk upon England's mountains green? And was the Holy Lamb of God on England's pleasant pastures seen? And did the Countenance Divine shine forth upon our clouded hills?" Etc..

43 Roman Invasion

The Romans are thought to have landed at Richborough in Kent and that there was no fighting when they landed. However, later, when they met opposition from the British the Romans were victorious at Rochester and Colchester, which became their capital town. They advanced through Britain capturing Iron Age forts like Old Sarum (see page 7 above) and eventually occupied most of England. They built very straight roads.

Stone Street, a Roman Road in Kent © and grateful thanks to Chas Phillips @IDrive.com

Roman Baths

Every Roman town had baths. They were for health and cleanliness – not swimming – and a visit was a social occasion.

Baths had three main rooms with different temperatures:

- Frigidarium – coldest
- Tepidarium – tepid
- Caldarium – hottest

After bathing, oils were rubbed into the skin, to replace the natural oils.

The Roman Baths in the City of Bath today

60 or 61 Boadicea (or Boudicca)

In 47AD, King Prasutagus died and the Romans arrested and flogged his widow, Boadicea. In 60, or 61 She led her tribe, the Iceni, in revolt against the Romans and many other Britons joined her because they resented the powerful Romans. The rebels took the towns of Colchester, St Albans and London but the Roman commander marched from Wales and defeated the Britons.

Religion under the Romans

The Romans worshipped many gods, including, gradually, the ruling emperor. Their gods included Jupiter, Juno, Vesta, Mars, Venus, Diana and Janus. The Romans punished all who refused to worship their gods. The Emperors Nero

(AD64) and Diocletian (AD300) persecuted Christians most fiercely. Many Christians were thrown to the lions or burnt or crucified. In about 305, St Alban was martyred. While it is by no means certain, this is recognised by St Bede as the date of the martyrdom of St Alban (the *Anglo-Saxon Chronicles* places it in 283). Alban was a convert from Paganism to Christianity in Roman Britain, and the first English Martyr. The cathedral at St Albans was founded in 793.

St Alban's Cathedral. With kind permission of David Kelsall©

In 313, the Emperor Constantine converted to Christianity and Christians were allowed to worship freely thereafter. The country of Wales became a stronghold of Christianity.

83 Battle of Mons Graupius

The Romans defeated the tribes of Albany (in effect present-day Scotland) at this Battle. It seems that nobody can quite work out where the site of this battle field lies.

122 Hadrian's Wall

Emperor Hadrian ordered the wall to be built: it was finished in 122. The wall was 73 miles long and stretched from Wallsend-on-Tyne to Bowness, near

Carlisle. It kept out the Picts, the inhabitants of Scotland. Every five miles or so there was a fort and every mile there was a mile castle, and between the mile castles there were two turrets.

Hadrian's Wall today. With kind permission of Newcastle Gateshead Initiative ©

The Antonine Wall, in Scotland, was built in 142 from the Forth to the Clyde for much the same purpose. The Pictish tribe that lived north of this wall were the Caledonii, hence the term Caledonian.

The Antonine Wall today. © Bill Mckelvie / Shutterstock.com

476 The Fall of the Roman Empire and the arrival of the Angles, Saxons and Jutes

The Romans had returned to Rome shortly after 400 to defend the rest of their empire and eventually the Roman Empire collapsed in 476. Barbarian and other tribes took over the lands they had conquered: Visigoths in Spain; Vandals in North Africa; Franks in France; Ostrogoths and Lombards in Italy; Angles, Saxons and Jutes in England.

The Saxons

In 449, King Vortigern invited two Saxon chiefs, Hengist and Horsa to defend Britain against raiders. The Saxons, a Germanic people, admired Britain and took over most of the land but not the western fringes. They were heathens and killed the priests and destroyed the Christian Churches. Their gods were:

Name:	The god of:
Woden	Wednesday
Thor	Thursday
Freya	Friday (Woden's wife)
Tiu	Tuesday
The Sun	Sunday
The Moon	Monday

The Saxons who remained on the continent were defeated by Charlemagne and converted to Christianity.

St Lawrence Chapel – a Saxon Chapel in Bradford upon Avon,(left).
St Mary Magdalen Saxon Church at Boveney near Windsor (right). The building shown is of 12th Century construction but there has been a church on this site since Saxon times.

Some maintain that the name Saxon is derived from "Sons of Isaac" and that they were one of the ten lost tribes of Israel.

The Angles and Jutes

The Angles came from the Angeln district of Schleswig in Germany. They settled in northern England but, in time, would form an Anglo-Saxon dynasty, ruling with a parliament or Witan (council of wise men). The Jutes, also from Germany, settled in Kent.

6^{th}C St Augustine

As we have just seen, the Saxons were heathen, but King Ethelbert's wife, Bertha, was a Christian from France. St Martin's Church in Canterbury is where Bertha heard Mass at that time.

St Martin's Church Canterbury today. © Dmitry Naumov / Shutterstock.com

When Pope Gregory (St Gregory the Great) saw some slaves in Rome that had been brought from Britain he was surprised to see children with fair hair and he asked who they were. When he heard they were Angles he is reported to have replied that they were "not Angles, but angels." And hearing that they were not Christian he sent Augustine (St Augustine of Canterbury) to Ethelbert. Augustine arrived in 597, he instructed Ethelbert who became a Christian with the result that Christian churches were built and the country gradually began to convert to Christianity with Augustine becoming the first Archbishop of Canterbury. As a result, Christianity spread throughout the land, although it should be noted that the Celtic churches in the Western fringes of the British Isles already practised Christianity, it having been introduced there shortly after Christ's Resurrection and possibly by St Joseph of Arimathea (see above – page 12). It should be borne in mind that British bishops were present at the Council of Arles in 314, and at Ariminum in 359, for instance.

St Augustine's Cross in Kent © Philip Halling with grateful thanks.

Augustine died in 604AD and when he died many lapsed from the faith.

St Brendan

St Brendan, an Irish monk, sailed west and is now generally believed to have discovered America, 1000 years before Christopher Columbus. After him, in about 1000AD, Leif Eriksson, son of Eric the Red (both Norwegians), is understood to have visited the north eastern coast of America; Eric the Red having visited Greenland.

664 Synod of Whitby

By way of background, and bearing in mind what you have just read, there were two strands of Christianity being practiced in Britain by the end of the 6th century. There was that strand which had been introduced by Augustine, direct from Rome, and the other long-established strand, the Celtic Church, in the western fringes. What this meant was that, over time, the Celtic Church had drifted away from some of the practices that Rome still adhered to and it therefore became necessary to make sure that both strands were totally united. That is what lies behind the importance of the Synod of Whitby.

One of these Celtic Christians was British born St Patrick, who had been responsible for the conversion of Ireland to Christianity by 450. In 563, an Irish monk, Columba, sailed from Ireland to the west coast of Scotland (possibly the island of Colonsay, but then north to) Iona where he set up a monastery. By the

time he died he had given Scotland its first Christian king in the person of Aidan.
In 635, Oswald, King of Northumbria, wanted the Word of Christ spread to his people.
He sent for Aidan in Iona, who, with a band of monks, set up a monastery at Lindisfarne, an island off the north-eastern coast of England.

Iona Abbey Today © Spumador / Shutterstock.com

Lindisfarne Abbey today. © Givi585 / Shutterstock.com

It was when they began to preach that it became apparent that the Celtic Church and St Augustine's Church (i.e. the Church of Rome) had different dates for

Easter. In 664, at Whitby (the Synod of Whitby), it was agreed to follow the Roman Church in this and other disciplinary matters.
St Hilda was the first Abbess of Whitby. Caedmon was a monk at Whitby – famous for his poetry.

Whitby and Whitby Abbey. © Oscar Johns / Shutterstock.com

687 Death of St Cuthbert

This Englishman evangelised most of Northumberland, was Bishop on Lindisfarne (Holy Island) and was buried in Durham Cathedral.

St Cuthbert is buried in Durham Cathedral. © Attila Jandi / Shutterstock.com

735 The death of the Venerable Bede

The Venerable Bede, or St Bede the Venerable as the Catholic Church calls him, was one of the first historians. He wrote "An Ecclesiastical History of the English People" – finished in 731 and still in print. He was a monk at Jarrow in north-east England.

790 Vikings

In 790, the Vikings attacked the east coast of Britain. They came from Norway and Denmark.

They murdered many of the people they encountered, especially Christians and destroyed the churches. The land they occupied, governed by their laws, was called Danelaw. The British prevented some of the attacks by paying the Vikings Danegeld – i.e. money, etc. – to go away, but this policy of appeasement didn't work (see Ethelred the Unready, page 24).

Visitors experiencing a ride through the Yorvik Viking Centre in York © www.coolplaces.co.uk

871 King Alfred

Alfred is the only king to be called "The Great". He defeated the Vikings under Guthrum, whom he persuaded to become a Christian. The battle was at Ethandune (Edington).

He was King of Wessex and held his parliament (or Witan) at Winchester, where he had been crowned. He and Guthrum signed the Treaty of Wedmore, dividing the country along Watling Street (i.e. Danelaw – Vikings to the north, Wessex to the south). He died in 899.

The Burnt Cakes episode followed Alfred's defeat at Chippenham. The story goes that, when fleeing for his life and seeking refuge in a homestead, the lady of the homestead, not knowing who he was, asked him to keep an eye on her cakes; a task he clearly failed to undertake – no doubt he was distracted by other greater concerns he had on his mind – and for which he was given a scalding by the unsuspecting lady

Other Danes, under the pirate Hastinga, attacked England, but Alfred beat them all off.

He founded the Royal Navy, the Army, many monasteries and schools, and a legal system. It was he that divided England into counties.

The Statue of King Alfred the Great in Winchester

8th C Offa's Dyke

In the 8th century, King Offa of Mercia, who was so powerful that he called himself King of the English, built a ditch to keep out the Welsh. It ran for 140 miles from the Dee to the Severn. It was 15 metres wide and can still be seen in many places.

Offa's Dyke today. Photo Rob Dingle, with grateful thanks©.

978 Ethelred the Unready

Ethelred was half-brother to St Edward the Martyr who had become King of England aged 12. Edward was murdered at Corfe Castle aged 15 in 978. Ethelred, aged 10, who did not murder his half-brother succeeded him but, in view of the murder, is reckoned to have usurped the Throne. Being so young, Ethelred was a weak king and in the hands of his advisors.

He tried to buy off the Danes by paying them money (Danegeld) to stop their attacks, but, "If once you have paid him the Danegeld, you never get rid of the Dane" (Kipling).

In 1013, the Danes under Sweyn overran England and Ethelred fled to Normandy.

Corfe Castle. © David Young / Shutterstock.com

1035 Death of King Canute

King Canute reigned from 1017-1035. He was a great king, but was not the Saint Canute of the same period. He was a Viking and was elected king after Ethelred's death and married Ethelred's widow, Emma of Normandy. The realm that he ruled over contained much of northern Europe. Canute went on a pilgrimage to Rome and is buried at Winchester.

1042 St Edward the Confessor

St Edward the Confessor reigned from 1042-1065. He was a monk at heart and planned Westminster Abbey. He lived in Normandy during Canute's reign. He had wanted to go on pilgrimage to Rome, but the Pope bade him build Westminster Abbey instead. He refused to pay Danegeld. He levied no taxes, paying for all public expenses himself. His reign was of unbroken peace and he is buried in Westminster Abbey.

1051 King Harold

(For family tree see Appendix 4a.)

In 1051, according to some reports, Edward had promised the English crown to William of Normandy and not Harold Godwinson and, apparently, Harold, son of Earl Godwin, who effectively governed the country on Edward's behalf, vowed to agree to William's succession.

However, when Edward died, Harold took the crown, being crowned the day after Edward died. Tostig, Harold's younger brother, also claimed the throne and asked Harald Hardrada, King of Norway, to assist him with troops. This force was defeated by King Harold at Stamford Bridge in Yorkshire on 25th September, 1066.

Meanwhile William had landed at Pevensea on 28th September 1066. King Harold marched 250 miles to meet William outside Hastings where the famous Battle of Hastings was fought on 14th October, 1066, with Harold being killed.

Before finishing this section it might be helpful to provide a brief summary of the 200 years leading up to the Norman Conquest:

9th to 11th Cs King Alfred to King Harold

King Alfred died in 899 and was buried in Winchester.

His son Edward and grandson Ethelstan, (both whom became became kings) recaptured most of Danelaw.

Ethelstan was succeeded by Edmund and then Eadwig.

King Edgar then reigned over all England from 959-975. I.e. the Kingdoms of Wessex, Mercia, Northumbria, Sussex, Kent, Essex and East Anglia were unified as the Kingdom of England from this time.

The suffix "sex" refers to lands which the Saxons had controlled (e.g. Essex, Sussex).

In 980, Viking attacks began again, but, as we have just seen, Ethelred the Unready tried to buy them off with Danegeld.
In 1013, Sweyn Forkbeard defeated Ethelred who fled to his brother-in-law in Normandy.
When Sweyn died, Ethelred returned with his son, Edmund Ironside. Sweyn's son, the heir to the throne, Canute, fled to Denmark.
When Ethelred and Edmund died, Canute returned to become King in 1017.
Canute rebuilt many churches and went to Rome on a pilgrimage.
When Ethelred died, his son, St Edward the Confessor, came from France to be King. He built Westminster Abbey.

Westminster Abbey, London. © Philip Bond LRPS CPAGB / Shutterstock.com

When St Edward The Confessor died in 1065 he is thought to have decreed that Harold Godwinson, an earl's son, should succeed him as king; but, as we say below, Harold Hardrada and William Duke of Normandy both had other ideas.

Step 3. Norman History (1066 to 1154)

1066 Battle of Hastings

(The build up to the battle is covered at the end of the previous step.)
This was fought on 14th October, 1066. At 9.30am the Norman invaders, on the lower ground, threw spears at the English, who threw stones back. The whole Norman army then advanced, but failed to break through. The Bretons on their left retreated; the English attacked them, but they were nearly all killed by the Bretons at the bottom of the hill.
A rumour that William had been killed led to him removing his helmet, to show he was still alive. The Normans fell back to regroup, whereupon the English, thinking they were retreating, attacked, but for a second time, many were killed. The Normans then outnumbered the English and when they attacked again, they won. Battle Abbey was built on the site.

Battle Abbey at the site of Battle of Hastings. © Andy Poole / Shutterstock.com

King William I

He reigned from 1066-1087. He organised the Domesday Book in 1086, and united the country of England. He died fighting in France and is buried at Caen.

Hereward the Wake

Hereward the Wake was an Englishman who fought against the Normans after the Conquest. He lived near Peterborough and joined forces with the Danes when they attacked that town. In 1071, William the Conqueror counter-attacked and defeated Hereward at Ely.

Norman Influence

Norman Castles: there are many fine examples still standing, especially the Tower of London, Windsor Castle and Dover Castle.

Even the smaller Norman castles, like that at Launceston in Cornwall, are very impressive.

The Normans built Motte and Bailey Castles. The motte was the mound, clearly seen in the above photograph, and the bailey was the enclosed and fortified courtyard.

Castles were usually built on hilltops but, if they were on flat ground they would have a moat and drawbridge. When the castle was attacked, everyone would gather inside.

The enemy might win a castle by starving out the occupants, or knocking the walls down with a battering ram.
Defending a castle was easier than attacking it because the defendants could be protected as they fired arrows or poured boiling lead on their attackers.
Life in a castle was not very comfortable for most therein.

Church building

Church-building began on a large scale (though Saxon churches already existed) and a few Norman churches still survive, such as at this fine example at Iffley just south of Oxford.

Monasteries & Cathedrals, such as Exeter and Salisbury were also begun during this period. (See more on church life and monasteries under the Plantagenet section.)
Under the Domesday Book, church dioceses were formed. (The counties had already been drawn up during Alfred's reign.)
Quarrying began and tin mining, which had been an important industry for well over one thousand years, became even more significant, especially in Cornwall and on Dartmoor.

The Bayeux Tapestry, which illustrates the various phases of the Norman Conquest, dates from this time.

Part of the Bayeux Tapestry © Jorvisco / Shutterstock.com

Certain place names are Norman such as Nottingham, Cambridge and Durham. We also note that funny sounding place names (such asAshby de la Zouche) are Norman, being a mixture of Old English and Norman. Not only was there a strong French influence, but the administration was done in Latin.

England was forged into one nation. The Normans pressed to invade Wales, but were resisted, mainly due to the strong leadership of Llewellyn I and II.
Saints' names were used instead of old English personal names.
Buildings began to be built of stone. Hence quarrying, to build the cathedrals and monastic institutions.

Towns expanded, particularly those with Norman castles, for example London (the Tower of London)

Tower of London © Salparadis / Shutterstock.com

1086 Domesday Book

When King William arrived in England there were few records and he did not know how much land he ruled. So he sent men all over the country to write down all the facts. Some of the people were angry because they did not want the King to know what they owned. They did not dare give the King's men wrong answers for fear of punishment. 1086 is the date of the Domesday Book and King William died in 1087.

1095 to 1099 First Crusade

The First Crusade took place from 1095-1099 (William Rufus' reign) and Peter the Hermit wandered through Europe preaching (advertising) the Crusade. The Crusaders assembled at Constantinople in 1096, crossed Turkey (Anatolia and Taurus Mountains) in 1097 and captured Antioch (1098). They captured Jerusalem (1099). The name *Crusade* comes from the Latin *crux* = cross. The First Crusade was the most important and successful Crusade.

The History of Jerusalem

After the Crucifixion, Jerusalem was destroyed in 70AD by the Romans who built a new city and banned the Jews from it. In 614, Jerusalem was captured by the Persians and in 638, a long period of Arab rule began which lasted until 1917. Jerusalem was held by the Crusaders between 1099 and 1187 (the Second Crusade, 1145-1149, resulted from the fall of the first Crusader state, Edessa). In 1917, it was governed by Great Britain, and in 1948, the British left and the Jews took over.

1097 Westminster Hall

Westminster Hall, the oldest building still standing on the site of the Palace of Westminster, was erected about this year. It is famous for both its age and its magnificent hammer beam roof.

11th Century The High Middle Ages

The High Middle Ages lasted from about 1050 to 1450 and during these years the Catholic Church dominated Europe. The Middle Ages themselves are generally reckoned to have lasted from 476AD (the Fall of Rome) to 1492AD, the discovery of America. The period between 476AD and 1050 is often referred to by the misnomer "the Dark Ages".

The word "Catholic" means "universal" from the Greek words "cath", throughout, and "holos", the whole. The word "mediaeval" is from the Latin for Middle Ages.

Achievements of the Catholic Church in the Middle Ages

In recent years there has been a tendency for anything mediaeval to be treated with scorn. However it is important to mention that many of the elements that we enjoy today, and which go to make up a civilized life, were developed during the Mediaeval Period, or the Middle Ages, such as:

- Under the Church a strong system of trading, commerce, markets, fairs and business centres developed.
- While some regard the first university as having been founded by St Patrick in Armagh, and that Oxford University was founded by Alfred the Great, universities, as we know them today, began to develop during this period, mainly as a result of the influence of St Dominic. Notwithstanding the claim by Salerno, near Naples, the earliest university is generally recognised as having been at Bologna (founded in 1088), followed by Paris (the College of the Sorbonne being founded in 1257, but earlier colleges pre-date it by a century), and (possibly earlier still) Oxford (where there is evidence of teaching as far back as 1096).

Oxford University today, seen from Boar's Hill

- Amongst the finest achievements of the period, during which nearly everyone in continental Europe was not only Catholic, but also a member of the Holy Roman Empire, were the Cathedral at Chartres, the *Summa Theologica* of St Thomas Aquinas and the life of St Francis of Assisi. The writings of St Thomas, who is sometimes known as the Dumb Ox, are recognised as being the pinnacle of Scholasticism, the enormously significant chapter of Western intellectual history.
- The Catholic Church encouraged scientific enquiry through the teaching of the *Quadrivium* (arithmetic, geometry, music and astronomy). Once students had mastered that, they were taught to relate their discoveries through the subjects of the *Trivium* (grammar, rhetoric and logic).
- Two of England's most enduring buildings were erected about this time: Westminster Abbey and Westminster Hall. The first was rebuilt by its holiest King, St Edward the Confessor, 1003-1066, and the latter by William II and Richard II.
- It is seldom realised that the great mediaeval cathedrals were also designed to be used as solar observatories, with particular regard to predicting the correct date for Easter.
- The Catholic Church started a system of inns for travellers, where accommodation was free.
- A monk, Eilmer, even built a glider which flew 600 feet in the eleventh century.
- During this time the following general improvements and innovations were also begun:
  - A system of warning ships about dangerous rocks at sea.
  - Improved agricultural practices, with improved breeds of cattle, they also established fisheries, particularly salmon fisheries. They developed the use of phosphates for fertilizer. This product came from iron production which resulted in high grade iron products. They were also highly skilled in forestry.
  - Agricultural land was provided at low rent to farmers on very long leases. After the Reformation such tenants were driven from their

land and made destitute. There were improved conditions for labourers, as Serfdom replaced Slavery. By the 14th century Serfdom was scarcely more onerous than a modern farm tenancy.

- Through monks and nuns, the church developed a universal health service through a system of building hospitals, one of which would be attached to every large church or religious house.
- The Church developed a universal system of comprehensive education.
- The Church also set up model factories and systems of social security and human rights. This was long before, and should not be confused with, the Declaration of the Rights of Man in 1789, which, rather than securing any human rights, was, in effect, a declaration of war against the Catholic Church.
- Wine production was another key development with Dom Perignon discovering how to make champagne.
- There were new systems for both national and international law and also of sound economics.
- Water power was also developed, which was used particularly in the production of cloth and leather goods.
- The Church also developed systems for waste disposal.
- Religious works of art and architecture from this time were without equal, and indeed still are.
- The Compass, which had been used as an aid to navigation in the second century BC, began to be used in earnest in the 13th century.
- Rules of warfare were introduced such as no fighting in Lent or on Sundays. Battles were organised on selected fields with the local peasants often continuing to work undisturbed next door.
- The Church developed the whole concept of charitable giving, such as the provision of alms houses for those who, through ill health or old age were unable to look after themselves. That system would be destroyed by Henry VIII at the time of the Reformation.

Fifteenth Century Alms House. This one is in Abingdon, near Oxford

In short, many regard the Catholic Church to have been the father of European civilisation. It civilized what had been a barbarous and chaotic continent. If one considers what it also achieved beyond Europe, it should explain why the Catholic Church is also now known as The Mystical Body of Christ.

11th – 14th Centuries The Cinq Ports

During this period five coastal towns in Kent and Sussex provided a navy for the defence of Britain. These were Hastings, new Romney, Hythe, Dover and Sandwich. Winchelsea and Rye were added later.

1100 Death of King William II

William the Conqueror had 3 sons, Robert, William and Henry. Robert displeased his father and so, when William I died, the crown passed to his second son William, who was not popular and became cruel. One day, when out hunting, he was hit in the chest by an arrow (now marked by the Rufus Stone in the New Forest).

Walter Tyrell, a close friend of the King, rode away after the death, but swore he was innocent. Was it an accident or murder? It was never decided.
William II had a red complexion and was nicknamed Rufus. He reigned from 1087-1100 and was succeeded by his brother Henry I.

Henry I

He was brother to William II and reigned from 1100-1135. He was known as Beauclerc, because he was so well-educated. It has been suggested that he might have been involved in William II's death. His son, William Adelin, was drowned in the White Ship on 25th November, 1120, which led to a succession crisis and a period of civil war called "The Anarchy."
He introduced the post of Chancellor of the Exchequer. He imprisoned his brother, Robert, for 28 years. He wanted his daughter, Matilda, to reign after him but his nephew thought otherwise. Henry died of a surfeit of lampreys.

1109 Death of St Anselm

He was born in Italy and lived from 1033-1109. He was a monk at Le Bec Hellouin, a Benedictine abbey in Normandy. He succeeded Lanfranc as Archbishop of Canterbury.
St Anselm advised William II, but his advice was not always taken and this was particularly the case in 1100 when Henry I ordered him to consecrate William Giffard Bishop of Winchester. Initially Anselm refused, an action which formed a part of the Investitures Dispute, but he later gave way. In due course Giffard was to restore Winchester cathedral with great magnificence.

The south aisle of Winchester Cathedral. The longest Gothic cathedral in Europe.

1135 King Stephen

He was a grandson of William the Conqueror and reigned from 1135-1154. He had promised Henry I that he would support Henry's daughter Matilda but he broke that promise. As a result, when he took the crown, Matilda waged civil war against him. On separate occasions they had each other imprisoned. His reign is referred to as "nineteen long winters". When he died, Matilda's son Henry became King Henry II.

1154 An English Pope

Nicholas Breakspear became the only English Pope, taking the name Hadrian IV (Adrian IV). He died in 1159.

Step 4. Plantagenet History (1154 – 1399)

1154 King Henry II

He reigned from 1154-1189. His mother was the Empress Mathilda.
He began the House of Plantagenet (from the Latin for the common broom shrub, worn by Geoffrey Anjou in his hat). He married Eleanor of Aquitaine, daughter of German King Henry V and wife of French King Louis VII. When he married, he controlled a large part of Europe from the Cheviots to the Pyrenees. He reorganised the country after the civil wars of Stephen's reign and was very powerful. He revised the law and made landowners pay scutage (shield money) for his army. His wife rebelled against him and she was imprisoned for 15 years at Salisbury. His successful reign was marred by the murder of St Thomas Becket.

1170 Henry II and St Thomas Becket

In mediaeval England, the Church and the State were very close. Henry II had appointed St Thomas á Becket as his Chancellor (the Head of the Law) and they were close friends.
In order to control the Church more closely, Henry appointed Thomas Archbishop of Canterbury. Thomas accepted, but, at the same time, and much to Henry's annoyance, Thomas resigned as Chancellor.
Thomas was lenient in his dealings with errant priests – too lenient, according to the King – so Henry drew up the Constitutions of Clarendon which, amongst other measures, decreed that priests be dealt with by the civil courts. Thomas refused to accept and left England. When he returned, he preached a sermon attacking heretics and some of his congregation complained about this to the King. The King replied: "Who will rid me of this turbulent priest?" and four knights understood this to mean that they should murder Thomas (1170), which they then did. Henry was aghast at the murder and walked barefoot to Canterbury, to pray at the spot where Thomas had been killed. A magnificent shrine was then erected in Canterbury Cathedral, but this was later destroyed under the orders of Henry VIII.

Canterbury Cathedral © Pawel Kowalszyk @ Shutterstock.com

1189 Richard I and the Crusades

Richard I was the eldest son of Henry II. He inherited the crown in 1189. Jerusalem was controlled by Muslims, whose leader was Saladin. The Pope granted indulgences to all who went on a Crusade to free Jerusalem. Richard led the Third Crusade, which landed at Jaffa and he joined the French King Philip Augustus.

They captured Acre, and won the Battle of Arsuf in 1191. Richard never reached Jerusalem, but returned home. He was killed fighting in France, in 1199.

Of his ten years on the throne, he spent just six months in England.

The statue of Richard III outside The Palace of Westminster in London

The Third Crusade

While the Crusaders were based in Jerusalem, they had to defend the city from the Muslims, who naturally wished to regain it. The Muslims, led by Saladin, eventually got their revenge by winning the Battle of the Horns of Hattin in 1187. A few weeks later, Jerusalem fell and the remains of the True Cross were lost. Europe responded by sending the Third Crusade (or Crusade of the Kings), 1189-1192. The German contingent, under Emperor Frederick Barbarossa, turned back after he had drowned at Seleucia.

King Richard I of England and King Philip II of France joined forces to attack Acre.

After they had beaten Saladin at the Battle of Arsuf (1191), Saladin gave permission for Christians to visit Jerusalem. Although the Crusaders were unable to hold Jerusalem they established a number of Crusaders States in and near the Holy Land. The most famous of these were The Kingdoms of Jerusalem, of Tripoli and of Antioch, but the Crusaders had been driven out of all of them by the Mamelukes from Egypt by the beginning of the fourteenth century.

Richard, who saw Jerusalem, but never entered it, did not besiege the city because he had no water supplies, but, even if he had taken it, with Saladin's great forces in Palestine, he would never have been able to hold it. Richard left for home, was shipwrecked and imprisoned in Austria, only to be released after his faithful minstrel Blondel found him and a ransom paid.

Richard I was not a popular king because he levied high taxes to pay for the Third Crusade.

While Richard was away, his brother John tried to take over the country.

Richard was very headstrong and upset both King Philip and the Duke of Austria.

He is buried with his parents (Henry II and Eleanor of Aquitaine) at Fontrevault.

1199 King John

He was Henry II's youngest son and reigned from 1199-1216.

He divorced his first wife and lived with Isabella of Angouleme.

He is reputed to have been fat, greedy and unjust.

He signed Magna Carta near Runnymede in 1215, an action which was the forerunner of English Justice.

The monument erected near Runnymede to commemorate the signing of Magna Carta

King John lost most of his lands in France and is often considered to have been England's worst King. He even lost his treasure while crossing a river near The Wash.

1215 Magna Carta signed

Magna Carta is regarded as the beginning of English Justice.

King John had made himself unpopular by imposing heavy taxes on the barons. The main tax was called scutage or shield money to pay for the army. The taxes were so heavy that the barons decided to make war on the King and only seven Barons took the King's side.

The King saw that he was outnumbered and he agreed to grant the barons the laws and liberties they wanted.

On 15th June 1215, at Runnymede, near Windsor, on the River Thames, he signed the great charter and thus the barons took over many of the responsibilities the King had formerly enjoyed.

The main points were:

I. No taxation without representation (i.e. the taxpayers would have some say in how their taxes should be spent).

II. Habeas Corpus ("that you may have the body"). This meant that nobody could be imprisoned without a fair trial.

An original copy of Magna Carta inside Salisbury Cathedral

On 1st November 2014 the European Union assumed a common system of European justice; a date that marked the demise of Magna Carta, the 800th anniversary of which was to be commemorated the following year.

Simon de Montfort

He was a Frenchman who married King Henry III's sister and was chosen by Parliament to lead their side in the quarrel with the King.
Parliament wanted to limit the King's power.
In 1264, Simon defeated and captured Henry III at the Battle of Lewes.
But in 1265, Simon was killed when he was defeated at the Battle of Evesham.
He is heralded as the first champion of parliamentary democracy.

1216 Henry III

Henry III reigned from 1216-1272. He was the eldest son of King John.
Aged only 9 at his father's death, he was brought up by priests.
He had a great love for churches and art (Salisbury Cathedral was built during his reign).
He rebuilt Westminster Abbey and the shrine of St Edward the Confessor.

St Edward the Confessor's Shrine in Westminster Abbey. © Dean and Chapter of Westminster

He tried to regain the French possessions his father had lost and he became very unpopular for the heavy taxes he raised.
The Barons, under Simon de Montfort, rebelled, but were eventually defeated at the Battle of Evesham in 1265.
During his reign, the first time Parliament was held, Canterbury Cathedral was finished, and many statues and stained glass windows created.
He is regarded as having been weak, but his reign ended with the country very peaceful.

Parliament

The word Parliament comes from the French "parler" – to speak. The first English parliament began shortly after Magna Carta (see 1215 and below, in this section). Before then, the King had made the laws and raised taxes. The

Church tried to influence the King, but when they disagreed, problems arose (viz. St Thomas á Becket (see page 39)).
When Henry III, son of King John, tried to raise heavy taxes, the barons under Simon de Montfort rebelled (see page 43). De Montfort imprisoned the King and summoned the first parliament in 1265.
In 1295, a different form of parliament was summoned called the Model Parliament.
Not only were knights called to Parliament, but also representatives from the towns, and two knights appointed from each shire (county). These formed the House of Commons.
In the 14th Century a new house began to emerge, the House of Lords. This so called Upper Chamber consisted of archbishops, bishops, abbots and priors (the Lords Spiritual) and noblemen (The Lords Temporal). Priors are superiors in a monastery who are lower in rank than an abbot and, being monks, this shows that many early members of the House of Lords were of lowly birth.
The House of Commons was responsible for raising taxes. This is why the House of Commons is more important than the House of Lords.
As war became more expensive, the House of Commons became even more important.

Battles

There developed four principles to be followed when fighting a battle. They are to:

1. Concentrate on the enemy's weak spot.
2. Surprise the enemy – pretend to do one thing, then do another.
3. Instil a sense of unity – your soldiers must all work together.
4. Ensure mobility – you must all be able to move quickly.

There is also luck to be expected such as at:

The Battle of Hastings in 1066:

- Harold's forces were exhausted.
- William arrived at the battle sooner than Harold expected.
- The Normans twice fell back to regroup, the English followed, thinking the Normans were retreating. The Normans turned and killed them (Harold was killed by a stray arrow).

The Battle of Evesham, 1265:

- De Montfort had put himself in a trap and Edward seized on the opportunity.
- The Welsh spearmen on De Montfort's side began to escape.
- De Montfort could not move.
- Luck – the heavy rain made fighting more difficult.

The Battle of Bannockburn, 1314:

- The English were tired and in a bad position with no retreat.
- The English did not all fight well together.
- The English could not use their archers.

Weapons

Up to 1400	1400 onwards
Chain mail	Armour plate
Warhorses	Warhorses
Sword	Sword
Large shield	Small shield
Battleaxe	Longbow
Feudal unpaid army	Paid professional soldiers
Scutage paid for other soldiers	
-	Explosives were used so that…
-	Thicker walls were needed for castles.
-	Heavy canons were made, such as Mons Meg.
-	Wars were thus more expensive, which led to…
-	More taxation needed to pay for the wars.
-	Parliament had to give authority for taxes to be raised.
-	Parliament thus became more powerful

1266 The Hebrides

Scotland gained the Hebrides from Norway at the treaty of Perth.

1272 Edward I

He reigned from 1272-1307.

He was the son of Henry III.

When his wife Eleanor of Castile died at Grantham, her body was taken to London and wherever it rested Edward erected a beautiful cross.

Charing Cross outside Charing Cross Station in London

Edward I took the Stone of Scone to Westminster Abbey. Scone was where the Scottish kings were crowned and Edward was thus trying to unite Scotland under his rule. The Stone of Scone used to lie underneath the Coronation Chair in Westminster Abbey

Coronation Chair © Dean and Chapter of Westminster

Note the void (above the two lions) where the Stone of Scone is placed at the time of a coronation

He created his eldest son, later Edward II, Prince of Wales, thus uniting Wales under his rule.
He introduced the long bow from Wales to his army and built magnificent castles in Wales, such as this one at Conway in North Wales.

Conwy Castle © Crown copyright (2015) Cadw

He went on a Crusade.
He reformed much of the law and agreed that parliament must approve tax-raising measures.
He was called "Longshanks" and "the Hammer of the Scots" for his victories over Scotland.
He is called Edward I because he was the first Edward to reign in England after the primogeniture system was established by the Normans (hence St Edward the Confessor is not called Edward I).

Welsh Castles

Castles were built along the Welsh border, such as Flint and Caerphilly.

Caerphilly Castle © Crown copyright (2015) Cadw

They were also built around the coast at Conway (now spelled Conwy, as we have just seen), Beaumaris, Caernarvon and Harlech.

Caernarvon Castle © Crown copyright (2015) Cadw

Harlech Castle © Crown copyright (2015) Cadw

Edward I used these magnificent castles and others to keep the Welsh in order.
Edward declared war on Llewellyn, Prince of Wales, in 1276, because he would not pay homage.
To fight the war he built castles around the coast and on hilltops.
In 1277, Llewellyn surrendered.
In 1282, Llewellyn rose again but was killed near Builth at the Battle of Orewin Bridge. After that, Edward expanded his castle-building programme.
These castles are the greatest mediaeval structures in Britain after the Cathedrals, etc.

Towns

Towns, though they grew in importance, during the Middle Ages were small.
In the year 1300, only 60,000 people lived in London, compared with 7 million today.
Fire was a great danger in the towns, where wooden houses and workshops were close together.

1277 Roger Bacon

Roger Bacon, an Oxford philosopher and mathematician, saw the need to reform the calendar, but was condemned for his novel ideas. He is credited with inventing the magnifying glass and gunpowder, and even foreseeing aeroplanes. He was also attracted to alchemy, the forerunner of chemistry, whose adherents sought to discover the supreme object of their cause, the philosopher's stone, a unique substance from which it was believed one could turn metals into gold. The mystical aspects of alchemy survive in esoteric movements such as Rosicrucianism.

1284 Cambridge University

The first college at this university, Peterhouse, opened its door to students, though the University itself dates to 1209.

With kind permission of the governors of Peterhouse, Cambridge ©

1290 Jews expelled from England

In 1290, the Jews were expelled from England by King Edward I, mainly because of their increasing antipathy over a number of centuries towards the Catholic Church. Their behaviour had so incensed the people that there had been riots. In one instance, St Hugh of Lincoln, as bishop, had intervened in defence of the Jews. It is now reckoned that a number of Jews remained in England, in spite of the expulsion order. Following their expulsion from England in 1290, in 1306 Jews were also expelled from France. Indeed the Jews were expelled from numerous countries over the centuries: the only place from which they were never expelled was Rome. The other reason given for these expulsions was their reluctance to be assimilated into their host country and embrace the Catholic Faith.

1300 First mechanical clock

One can see what claims to be the oldest, still working, in Salisbury Cathedral.

Mappa Mundi

This is the date normally ascribed to the drawing of the Mappa Mundi (map of the world) of which there are many copies but the most famous is to be found in Hereford Cathedral

Mappa Mundi © Hereford Cathedral.org

Hereford Cathedral © freedom100m / Shutterstock.com

1305 William Wallace executed

Sir William Wallace, a Scottish patriot, led a revolt against the English and defeated them at Stirling in 1297, assuming the title of Governor of Scotland. However the English King, Edward I, defeated him at Falkirk in 1298 after which Wallace was captured and executed in London.

Reivers

From about this time to the beginning of 17th century there was constant raiding across the border between England and Scotland. The raiders from both sides were called Reivers.

A tower on the borders on England and Scotland for watching out for raids by Reivers. © Stock Solutions / Shutterstock.com

1307 Duns Scotus dies

Duns Scotus, whose extraordinary erudition and intellectual skill earned him the title *Doctor Subtilis* ("Subtle Doctor"), was a great Scottish Franciscan philosopher.

Problems in the Church in the High Middle Ages

In spite of its position of huge influence, Rome fell into anarchy in 1303 and the Papal Court was moved to Avignon in 1305, until, after the Great Schism, St Bridget of Sweden and St Catherine of Siena helped resolve the schism and influenced the return of the Papacy to Rome in 1417.

Edward II

He was the son of Edward I and reigned from 1307-1327.
He married Queen Isabella, daughter of Philip IV of France.
He lost the Battle of Bannockburn, 1314.
He was murdered (gruesomely) by Roger Mortimer at Berkeley Castle, Mortimer having taken Queen Isabella as his mistress.

Berkeley Castle © David Hughes / Shutterstock.com

Edward was buried at Gloucester Cathedral.

1314 Battle of Bannockburn

After Edward I's death in 1307, the Scottish King, Robert the Bruce, began to drive the English out of Scotland. By 1314, Stirling Castle was the only English outpost in Scotland.
When the English arrived near the castle to relieve it, Sir Henry de Bohun rode forward to kill the unprotected Bruce, but Bruce killed him.

The two sides fought all day and the English camped close to the Forth that night.
The next day, 24th June, Robert charged the English who were hemmed in and unable to use their Archers. When the Scottish small folk, local farmers, etc., appeared at the end of the day, the English will was broken and the battle lost.

The Statue of Robert the Bruce at Bannockburn. © Heartland arts / Shutterstock.com

1320 Declaration of Arbroath

The Scots claimed their independence from England.

1327 Edward III

Edward III was the son of Edward II and reigned from 1327-1377.
He was married to Philippa of Hainault.
He imprisoned his mother at Castle Rising for 28 years.

Castle Rising © Leslie Rigg / Shutterstock.com

He began the Hundred Years War in 1338:

- to gain the French crown.
- to expand the wool trade.
- to expand the wine trade.

He won the following battles:

- Sluys, 1340.
- Crecy, 1346 – with long-bows.
- Poitiers, 1355.

In 1348, the Black Death ravaged the country and killed his daughter Joan.
His campaigns, while successful, never resulted in him gaining the French throne.
He rebuilt Windsor Castle and created the Order of the Garter, and his most famous sons are:

- The Black Prince, the father of Richard II.
- John of Gaunt, the father of Henry IV.

The Black Prince

He was the son of Edward III who died in 1376, before his father.
He was brave, and a tough soldier who won many battles for his father, including, in 1356, the battle of Poitiers where he captured the French king.
He died before Edward III and so never became King. On his father's death in 1377, the Black Prince's son, Richard, was crowned Richard II.
He was born in 1330 and joined the Hundred Years War in 1346.
Edward, the Black Prince, "won his spurs" at Crecy in 1346. The French cavalry and crossbowmen were no match for the English long-bow.
He is called the Black Prince from the colour of the livery worn by his retainers.
In 1361, he married "The Fair Maid of Kent," Princess Joan.
His tomb is in Canterbury Cathedral.

1337 The Hundred Years War

The Hundred Years War began in 1337 when England, which claimed half of France, also claimed the French throne. The French who wanted to govern themselves won in the end (by 1453) even though the English won notable battles at Crecy (1346), Poitiers (1356) and Agincourt (1415).

1346 The Battle of Crecy.

It was fought on 26th August 1346

The English defeated a much larger French army.

It was one of the major battles of the Hundred Years War.

Edward III claimed the French throne.

The French Army was led by Philip VI and pursued the English, who crossed the Somme near Abbeyville.

Edward had Welsh and English longbows.

Philip had Genoese crossbows – which had to be rewound.

Many French fought on horses, so when their horses were killed they were unable to get up and fight in their armour.

There was a violent thunderstorm.

The Black Prince sent to his father for help. His father replied "let the boy win his spurs."

Edward then marched on Calais.

1348 The Black Death

In 1348, a terrible plague swept Europe from China.

It was carried by rats travelling in merchant ships.

Sufferers could die within hours.

It was highly contagious.

It affected the groin, armpits and skin. It could cover a man with black boils.

Many priests died giving the last rites. With the religious houses needing replacement priests, many were poorly trained and their poor standard is thought to have been used popularly, and largely retrospectively, to justify the Reformation.

Nearly half the British population died.

Afterwards, in 1351, there were many fewer men to work the land and these demanded higher wages which led to the Peasants' Revolt in 1381. It also led to the end of the Feudal system.

In the 14th Century, there were no drains and little attention was paid to personal hygiene.

Fleas are believed to have spread the disease from the rats.

With more work to be done, the villains began to wander from their lords, seeking others to whom they might pay rent – rather than working for them. Pope Clement VI gave permission for laymen to minister to the dying during the Black Death.

1377 Richard II

He reigned from 1377-1399.
He was the son of the Black Prince.
He bravely stood against the Peasants' Revolt and stopped it.
His uncle was the Duke of Lancaster, John of Gaunt.
He married Anne of Bohemia, who died, and, later, Isabella, but had no children.
He was unpopular with Parliament because he ignored it.
Henry Bolingbroke, John of Gaunt's son, took Parliament's side and imprisoned Richard.
In 1399, Richard abdicated and died (was he murdered?) in 1400.
Henry Bolingbroke became Henry IV.

1381 The Peasants' Revolt

This revolt took place in 1381.
It was led by Wat Tyler and John Ball – a priest.
One of John Ball's famous quotes being, "When Adam delved and Eve span, who was then the gentleman?"
The march on London resulted from a combination of factors:

- Black Death (1348) had led to great depression.
- Tyler & Ball taught that rebellion would bring riches to the poor.

The Hundred Years War had led to a poll tax which everyone had to pay equally.
Wat Tyler was killed when the peasants reached London, but the King, Richard II, bravely quietened the masses.
With their leader dead, the crowd went home, but the poll tax was abolished and the peasants were given more freedom and money.
During the revolt, Wat Tyler's men murdered the Archbishop of Canterbury in St John's Chapel in the Tower of London.

In the 1980s, a Poll Tax (this time it was called the Community Charge) was reintroduced, causing riots and unrest, but it too failed and was abolished in 1993.

1382 Winchester College founded

This is the oldest established public school in Britain

Winchester College in College Street, Winchester

Life and times in the Middle Ages

This was a time when the whole of Britain was Catholic and life revolved around the Catholic Church. It would therefore be helpful to describe some aspects of what that life would have been like. With monasteries dominating the land it would be sensible to start with monks and friars.

Monks and Friars

Monks live in monasteries, such as Benedictine, whereas Friars (such as the Franciscans (the Greyfriars)) are members of mendicant (begging) religious orders, some of whose members, when not living in Friaries, travel the countryside doing pastoral work, preaching, etc., and often become missionaries abroad. A monk remains principally within his monastery.

Monastic Houses include:
Benedictines, Cistercians (who also follow the Rule of St Benedict) and Carthusians (though technically these are hermits with elements of common life).

The Cistercian Abbey of Rievaulx today with kind permission of the National Trust©

Mount Grace Priory (Carthusian) today, with kind permission of the National Trust ©

The monasteries that dominated the countryside were usually Benedictine (the model for them originating in Monte Cassino). During their time the monks kept records of all that happened – they were historians. They copied the writings of the learned men from earlier centuries – hence illuminated manuscripts.

The Dragon (Serpent) and the Woman of the Sun.
Courtesy of the British Library©
http://www.bl.uk/catalogues/illuminatedmanuscripts/TourPopup.asp?TourID=244

They organised the first hospitals; they welcomed strangers, looked after the poor and needy and organised the teaching of children.

Orders of Friars include:
Franciscans (Greyfriars), Dominicans (Blackfriars), and Carmelites (Whitefriars – from the outer cloak of their habit), founded on Mount Carmel in Palestine by St Berthold in 1154, though claiming a lineage back to Elias. Carmelites are the most contemplative of the friars.

Contemplative Orders for women include:
Poor Clares (an order of Franciscan nuns founded by St Clare of Assisi) and Carmelites (the female order is enclosed and contemplative). St Teresa of Avila and St John of the Cross reformed the Carmelites (both female and male) to become discalced, or barefoot (in fact they wear sandals), though the primitive order of Carmelites also continued to exist as monks and friars

A typical day in a Monastery

It would usually follow this schedule:

Midnight	Matins
1.00am	Lauds
1.30am	Bed
6.00am	Prime
6.30am	Chapter – spiritual instruction/discussion & Parliament – business discussion
7.00am	Mass for workers and priest's private Masses
7.30am	Light breakfast (mixtum)
	Work and/or Lectio Divina (spiritual reading)
9.00am	Tierce
9.15am	Conventual High Mass
10.00am	Work
12.00pm	Sext
12.15pm	Dinner (and recreation)
3.00pm	None
3.15pm	Work
6.00pm	Vespers
6.30pm	Collation (supper)
7.30pm	Compline
8.00pm	Bed

Chivalry

In the middle ages men were taught to live in accordance with three main aims:

- strength in war
- devotion to religion
- good manners

This was called the Age of Chivalry, mainly from the 11th-15th Centuries.
Chivalry comes from chevalerie or armoured knights on horseback.
Boys, at the age of 7, would become pages in noble households, learning riding, singing, good manners, music, Latin, French, reading and writing.
At age 14 they would become squires to a knight, learning to be soldiers and helping their knight to manage all his affairs including his horses.

At age 21, if they could afford it, they became knights (see below) and were granted land in return for military service.
They kept fit by taking part in Tournaments.

Knighthood

In battle, a squire would be knighted by being touched on the shoulder with a sword (dubbed).
In preparation for a peacetime dubbing he would:

- serve his lord at dinner
- have his head shaved
- bathe
- be reminded of his duties
- spend the night in prayer
- confess his sins to a priest
- hear Mass
- dress in rich clothes
- receive sword and spurs – signs of knighthood
- be dubbed

These were called Knights of the Bath.
Some knights formed themselves into religious orders, such as Knights Hospitallers (to feed, shelter and heal pilgrims) or Templars (to protect the Christian shrines and churches in Jerusalem, as well as the Temple, and protect pilgrims). Knights belonging to no order are Knights Bachelor.

The relationship between England and France in the Middle Ages

English and French affairs were closely connected because the first Kings of England were also Dukes of Normandy. The English monarchs lost Normandy in 1204, but continued to be involved with France, because they had other lands in the South. But by 1453, all French lands, except Calais, had been lost. Nonetheless, the two countries traded with each other, in wine and wool.

Crafts and Guilds

Workers in each trade formed organisations called guilds (from Old English, geld = payment).

Those workers with special skills belonged to a craft guild.
They would meet in the guildhall in the local town.
Workers in the same trade usually worked near each other. In York, the butchers worked in The Shambles.

The Shambles in York © Shanna Hyatt / Shutterstock.com

The guilds insisted on high standards. The Church insisted on just prices.
A worker wanting to join a craft guild first became an apprentice, then a journeyman (because he could do a day's work) and then after making a "Masterpiece", if the masters of the guild accepted it, he became a skilled craftsman.
The guilds would perform mystery plays to entertain and teach the people in the town.
Each guild performed acts of charity:

- looking after sick members
- looking after widows and children

- praying for the souls of their members
- supporting their local church/guild chapel/chantry

Fairs and Markets

The word "fair" comes from the Latin *feria* for "day" (holy day).
The fairs were held in church grounds on the days of their local saint's feast, or other holydays and tradesmen from far and wide would come to sell their goods.
Tavistock's Goosey Fair (for example) began in the 13th Century.
Fairs were held from time to time throughout the year, and the tradesmen, sometimes from abroad, would travel from town to town for the different fairs.
The word "market" comes from the Latin *mercatus* = merchant. Markets were (and still are) held regularly every week or month in many towns.
In town markets, local tradesmen and farmers, etc., set up stalls to sell their goods.
The town is paid a sum, for the space a stall occupies, by the stall-holder.

Feudalism

Feudalism is a system of ownership of land. Large estates were called manors and the noble in charge was called a lord. The lord would allow certain men to hold their land in return for serving in the lord's army when required. This man was called a vassal.
The ceremony at which the vassal was granted the land was called "homage".
Those who worked on the land were called serfs or villains.
The serfs lived in poor houses clustered near the lord's castle – hence village.
The lord sometimes granted the inhabitants of a village or town freedom to organise life in the town as they wished. The details were recorded in a Charter.

Gothic Style

It originated in France in the 12th Century.
It is marked by: pointed arches, graceful columns, tall spires and decorations (tracery).
Gothic buildings in Britain date from 1200-1500.
This period is divided into:

- Early English – simple design – Salisbury Cathedral

- Decorated – decorations – Exeter Cathedral
- Perpendicular – more solid – Eton College Chapel.

Early English Architecture – Salisbury Cathedral ©martinjamescook / Shutterstock.com

Decorated Style – Exeter Cathedral © Ian Woolcock / Shutterstock.com

Perpendicular Style – Eton College Chapel

The earliest example of gothic architecture in England is at Canterbury Cathedral.

The most famous gothic cathedrals are Notre Dame in Paris and at Chartres. Most gothic sculpture was destroyed at the Reformation.

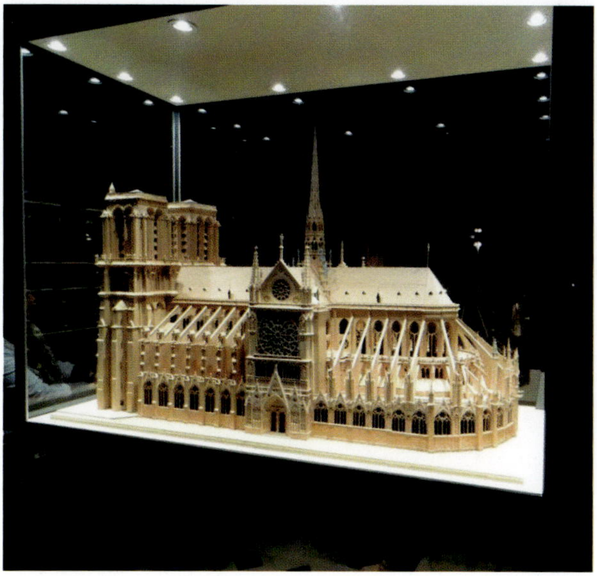

The model of Notre Dame Cathedral which can be seen inside that cathedral

Transport and Travel

In mediaeval times, travellers used the old Roman Roads – none had been built since.

Few carts existed, so goods were carried by pack horse.

Wealthy people rode, the rest walked.

Travel was dirty and dangerous.

Ships were used for transport, now that the rudder had been invented. They were also much larger vessels and could sail against the wind.

Tournaments

Tournaments were held to keep the knights fit, as well as for entertainment. They included:

- jousting – 2 knights on horseback charging each other with blunt lances
- tilting – a knight would charge a model (manikin) soldier, hit him with a lance and try to avoid being hit by a bag of sand which would swing around behind him
- melee – a pitched battle between knights
- list – a long wooden enclosure in which to hold the joust.

Tournaments could be very dangerous.

Jousting © Lovell / Shutterstock.com

Warwick Castle, where jousting can still be seen being re-enacted today

Pilgrimage

The Catholic Church teaches that it is a purifying thing to visit the bodies of the Saints and, above all, the places of martyrdom. A pilgrimage remits sins and is a penance. Going on a pilgrimage helps to develop character.

An early English ballad says of those who go on a pilgrimage, such as, in those days, to the shrine of St Thomas Becket in Canterbury Cathedral – later destroyed on the orders of King Henry VIII:

"They bear with them no manner of thing
That was worth a farthing
No cattle, no gold, no fee
But meekly they asked their meat
Wherever they might it get
For Holy Charity."

Pilgrims wore a special smock and hat, carried a stick and wore pilgrim signs, which often enabled them to pass through hostile land. Pilgrims to Canterbury wore a bell or the head of a Saint on a brooch. Their wallet was their scrip.

Both Canterbury and Winchester have grown as a result of their being places of pilgrimage.

Pilgrims often dictated the course of roads. They wore out a path from the sea coast to Canterbury.

Crusades arose from the idea of pilgrimage to the Holy Land. Some pilgrims went in search of miracles and cures.

Miracle plays are derived from returning pilgrims acting out their pilgrimage for the benefit of those unable to visit the shrine, etc. (vide the Passion plays at Oberammergau).

International Communications owe an enormous debt to pilgrimages.

Pilgrimages were the only reasons that led people to visit another country peacefully.

An exceedingly large number of foreigners came to visit the tomb of the Holy Blissful Martyr, St Thomas of Canterbury (St Thomas Becket).

Pilgrims often carried "the mails" and caused wayside inns to be set up.

Religious orders were founded to protect pilgrims (Knights Templar).

Dangers/Scandals of Pilgrimages:

It is wrong to (i) insist that pilgrimages are necessary for salvation; (ii) go on a pilgrimage and neglect home duties or, (iii) go on a pilgrimage and live wantonly.

Particular Pilgrimages:

(a) Westminster: (St Thomas Becket suggested the building of the magnificent shrine to St Edward the Confessor)

(b) Canterbury:

- birthplace of Anglo-Saxon Christianity

- scene of Martyrdom of St Thomas Becket
- Henry VIII only declared himself head of Church of England after he had personally attacked St Thomas and strongly discouraged pilgrimages
- Chaucer says one should visit in Spring "the Holy Blissful Martyr for to seek."

For pilgrimages to Canterbury, pilgrims would gather in Winchester, Dover and London.

(c) Winchester:

- had been the spiritual centre of England until the martyrdom of St Thomas
- St Swithin's shrine

The west façade of Winchester Cathedral

(d) Salisbury:

- there is a prayer for pilgrimage in the Sarum Missal.
- St Osmund's shrine

Step 5. The Houses of Lancaster and York (1399 – 1485)

1399 The Hundred Years War (continued from 1337 above)
The war had begun during the reign of Edward III and lasted spasmodically from 1337 until 1453.
There were few great battles and the French were victorious in the end.
Since 1066, English Kings had been Dukes of Normandy, and, under Henry II, England had controlled large areas of France. The French resented this and the Hundred Years War was their means of getting rid of the English.
The war began when Philip VI of France attacked the English in Aquitaine.
Edward III sent two armies, one to Aquitaine and the other to northern France.
Because the English were successful, the French sent a large army, in 1346, to northern France, to stop their advance. The English defeated them at Crecy.
In 1356, the French were again defeated at Poitiers, but with Edward III old, the Black Prince ill, and France with a new young King, the tide then turned.
In 1415, England had a new King in Henry V and he defeated the French at Agincourt and gained control of most of northern France, including Paris.
In 1431, the martyrdom of St Joan of Arc, coupled with weak English leadership, gave the French new courage.
The French gradually pushed the English out of France, finally defeating them at Formigny in 1450. This is commonly regarded as being the final battle of the Hundred Years War but there are those who say that the final battle was actually The Battle of Bosworth.

The Main Dates:
1340 Battle of Sluys – English Naval Victory
1346 Battle of Crecy – English victory by longbow
1356 Battle of Poitiers – English capture French king
1415 Battle of Agincourt – English victory by longbow
1450 Battle of Formigny – French victory

Death of John of Gaunt
(For his family tree see Appendix 4b.)
He lived from 1340-1399.

"Gaunt" was how the English pronounced Ghent in Belgium, where he was born.
He fought in the Hundred Years War, but not very successfully.
His first wife bought him the Dukedom of Lancaster. He was thus father of the Lancastrians in the Wars of the Roses.
His second wife, Constance of Castile, gave him and his successors close unity with Spain.
His fame is really because he was father and grandfather of three kings, although not a king himself.

King Henry IV (formerly known as Henry Bolingbroke.)
He reigned from 1399-1413.
He organised the abdication of his first cousin Richard II.
The main event in his life was when the Earl of Northumberland, his son Hotspur and the Archbishop of York rose against him. Henry IV defeated them at the Battle of Shrewsbury in 1403.
It was his dirty work in organising the abdication of Richard II that led to the Wars of the Roses in 1455.

1413 Henry V
He reigned from 1413-1422.
He tried valiantly to pursue Edward III's right to the French throne.
His greatest victory was winning the Battle of Agincourt in 1415.
He died of dysentery when he was 35.

1415 Battle of Agincourt
Agincourt is in northern France; the battle took place in 1415.
6,000 Englishmen, under Henry V, defeated 20,000 Frenchmen.
The English longbow men, who were highly skilled, were far more effective than the heavily armoured French knights.

1416 Death of Owen Glendower
He lived from 1359-1416 and was of royal Welsh blood.

A local argument grew into a revolt against the English (1400). Owen's forces attacked many Welsh castles, many surrendered, but Caernarvon, with 28 men, held out.
In 1405, Prince Henry, later Henry V, slowly began to defeat him.

Lollards

Lollards were the first of what may be termed Protestants (there were many heretics prior to them). Their leader was John Wycliffe who died in 1384.
They protested against:

- the Pope's powers
- confession of one's sins to a priest
- the wealth of the Church

They were thus also heretics and many were burned at the stake.
When Wycliffe died, his followers, under John Hus, kept the movement alive. This contributed to a movement that was to become the Reformation. There was a small rebellion of Lollards in 1414.

1422 Henry VI

He reigned twice: 1422-1461 and 1470-1471.
He was crowned King of France (as well as England), but this title disappeared in 1435.
His reign is confused and dominated by the Wars of the Roses (1455-1485).
He founded Eton College in 1440 and King's College, Cambridge.

Statue of Henry VI in School Yard at Eton College

Henry's reign was interrupted by Edward IV, his third cousin and a great-great grandson of Edward III. Henry was imprisoned in the Tower of London from 1465-1470 and it is believed that he was murdered, possibly while at prayer. (See also Wars of the Roses.) For many years after his death he was revered as a saint.

1431 Death of St Joan of Arc

She received visions while at home that the English, who were besieging Orleans in France, would be defeated and that the Dauphin would be crowned. After questioning her, the Dauphin agreed to let her dress as a boy in armour. She set out for Orleans with the French army and relieved the siege. During this siege the French attacked a convoy bringing provisions to the English forces and the French were defeated at what is known as the Battle of the Herrings. The Dauphin, Charles, was crowned in Rheims in 1429.
The war continued; Joan was captured by the English and burnt at the stake for (unfounded) heresy, as a result of a partisan trial (later annulled), much being made of her wearing men's clothes, which she argued was necessary for her role in battle, behind enemy lines, but also to preserve her chastity. She was later exonerated and canonised. She is patron of France.

1455 The Wars of the Roses

(For family tree see Appendix 4d)
The wars started in 1455, when Henry VI's third cousin Richard Duke of York challenged him for the throne at the first Battle of St Albans. Henry VI lost, thus giving York the crown.
Henry VI was a devout King who had suffered a stroke. While he was ill, Richard had been protector. Now he was better, Richard did not want to hand control back.
Henry VI soon escaped the clutches of the Duke of York and his main supporter, the Earl of Warwick.
In 1460, Warwick defeated Henry at Northampton and Richard appeared free to keep the throne.
But Richard was killed by supporters of the Queen (Margaret).
Warwick was then defeated at the second Battle of St Albans.

Warwick fled to Hereford and defeated the Queen's forces at Mortimer's Cross in 1461, whereupon Owen Tudor, a supporter of Henry VI, was beheaded.
Owen Tudor had married Henry V's widow, Queen Margaret, and was grandfather of Henry VII.
The defeat at Mortimer's Cross, was a defeat for Henry VI and so Edward (Richard Duke of York's son) was crowned Edward IV .
After his Coronation, Edward and Warwick marched north and defeated Queen Margaret's forces at Towton in 1461.

Summary (1455-1461):

- Richard of York challenges Henry VI of Lancaster
- they fight four battles, Richard is killed
- Henry is defeated and Richard's son Edward becomes Edward IV giving apparent victory to the House of York.
- subsequent events and discoveries were to prove that Edward was illegitimate.

Paston Letters

These represent correspondence between the Paston family from 1422-1509. They are a unique collection of papers which describe life in mediaeval England. They show how unsettled English life was during the Wars of the Roses.

Warwick the King Maker

The Earl of Warwick was very powerful.
He began by supporting Richard Duke of York and was thus a supporter of Edward IV.
However, by 1470, Edward was growing unpopular, because he asked too much of his supporters. They turned against him and he was forced to surrender.
Warwick tried to run the country but failed to gain support. He thus released Edward IV, but it was Edward who took control, not Warwick.
Warwick & Clarence (Edwards's brother) tried to oppose Edward by stirring up rebellions, but they failed and fled to Normandy.

Once there, they resolved to enlist the support of Henry VI who was in the Tower.
When Warwick & Clarence returned, Edward was unable to resist them and it was Edward's turn to flee to France (1470).
When Edward IV returned in 1471, with Richard (III), Warwick was unable to muster enough support, Clarence joined Edward, and Edward reclaimed the throne, putting Henry VI back in the Tower.

1461 Edward IV

He reigned from 1461-1483.
He was the victor of the Wars of the Roses.
His claim to the throne was based on the fact that Henry IV had no right to take it from Richard II. However, subsequent discoveries, including some in 2002, have clearly indicated that Edward IV was himself illegitimate.
During his reign, printing began – William Caxton.
He was secretly married before he married Elizabeth Woodville. His children were thus illegitimate and it is this that caused Richard III so much trouble.

1476 Printing and other discoveries

Printing began in China (perhaps) long before it came to Europe. It was brought to England by an Englishman, William Caxton, who became interested in it in Belgium, in 1476.The reason he was so successful in introducing it into England is because he worked for Edward IV's sister. Thus Caxton did not invent printing but he encouraged its use in England. The most famous European book of the 15th century is the Guttenberg Bible. There is a copy at Eton College and one on public display at the British Library.

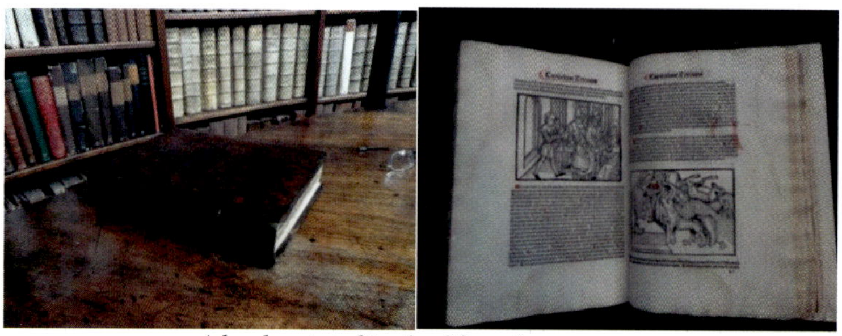

A book printed in the fifteenth century –
by kind permission of the archivist at the Birmingham Oratory ©

The Mediaeval Town

Towns grew up mainly because of trade.
Many were established near bridges or crossroads.
Some towns were granted a charter for running their own affairs.
The main trade was in wool and wine.
Inns were built for travelling traders and pilgrims.

1483 Richard III

(For family tree see Appendix 4d. You *are* advised to look at this since the relationships of everyone involved in this fascinating period of history are very complicated. A clear head is needed!)
He was born at Fotheringhay Castle and reigned from 1483-1485.

All that remains of Fotheringhay Castle today

Richard was Edward IV's younger brother.
For centuries Richard III has been given a bad reputation, especially with regard to the mysterious disappearance of "The two little princes", see Appendix 4d. For example there is this famous derogatory rhyme believed to come from the period and which goes "The Cat (Catesby), the Rat (Ratcliffe) and Lovell the dog, now all rule England under Richard the hog" (Richard's heraldic symbol was a white boar.)
However, over recent decades, his bad reputation has been seriously questioned, especially by those who consider that history tends to be written by "the winners". In this case, the winners, the Tudors, if they were to consolidate their power, needed to blacken Richard's name, and this they very successfully did.

These are the facts that Richard's supporters now assert:

- He was born with no expectation of becoming king.
- There are no contemporaneous reports of him having a withered arm or twisted back. (See also final point below.)
- When Edward IV died, Edward's widow (Elizabeth Woodville), wanting her son, Edward V to reign, tried to block Richard III (the boy's uncle) from becoming Protector. However the Royal Court wanted otherwise so Richard was indeed appointed Protector and a short time later, crowned king.
- In 1483 it was announced that Edward IV's marriage to Elizabeth had been bigamous. This meant that Edward V was illegitimate and could not inherit the throne. So it is no surprise that the Royal Court naturally proclaimed Richard king.
- The conjecture is that, once the Woodville's had been defeated over the succession, they devised a plan, with French help, to install Henry Tudor (Richard III's 5th cousin) and then marry Henry to Elizabeth, the daughter of Edward IV's illegitimate marriage to Elizabeth Woodville.
- If you turn to Appendix 4d, you will see that it's highly likely that Edward IV was himself also illegitimate.

As already mentioned, one of the biggest issues concerning Richard III is that of the two little princes, Edward V and his brother Richard Duke of York, who both disappeared in 1484.
Did Richard murder them?

- By all accounts Richard was a loyal, brave, pious and just person; not a murderer.
- He had no motive to kill them once he was rightfully king.
- Lawyers, politicians, investigators and psychologists have declared that, with no motive to kill them, and no opportunity of doing so, he is not the prime suspect. Apart from anything else, to murder two princes in the Tower of London, a place that employed 600 people, and get away with it, would have been impossible.

Other facts about Richard III's short reign:

- He appointed Lord Hastings to be his Chancellor, but when Hastings plotted against Richard with the Dowager Queen, Elizabeth Woodville, Richard ordered his execution.
- There are copious reports of him being a great king, who was extremely popular, dispensed justice fairly to all classes in society and who was also praised by priests. Bishop Langton said of Richard "I have never liked the condition of any prince as well as his."
- He achieved a great deal in his two year reign.
- Henry Tudor landed in 1485 at Milford Haven and met and defeated Richard at Bosworth that year. Henry was crowned Henry VII.
- Richard's buried body was discovered in a car park in Leicester in 2012. He had no withered arm and, with the spine originally diagnosed as hunchbacked (kyphosis) upon excavation, this distortion had occurred because the body had been buried in a grave that was far too short for it. It was later confirmed that the king suffered from scoliosis (meaning that one of his shoulders was higher than the other – a common occurrence – a condition even shared by record-breaking sprinter Usain Bolt) and not kyphosis. This means that we can dismiss the tendency to refer to him as hunchbacked.

1485 Battle of Bosworth

There has been some dispute in recent years over the exact area where the Battle of Bosworth was fought. This photograph taken at the Bosworth Heritage Centre looks north to the site of the (now-believed) battle site a mile or two away.

Henry Tudor, with no strong claim to the throne, opposed Richard III, having landed at Milford Haven.
Lord Stanley, with a large private army, was asked by Richard to help him. Richard apparently threatened Stanley's son with death if he didn't help. Stanley decided to support Henry. However, even then, the battle was very even. But when Richard was killed, his cause was ended and his followers fled. Henry was crowned unofficially on the battlefield as Henry VII.
He consolidated his remote claim to the throne by marrying Elizabeth of York, the Woodville daughter of Edward IV.
To repeat what has already been mentioned, some say that, since the battle of Bosworth was won by Henry Tudor with substantial French backing, it was, in effect, the last battle of the Hundred Years War.

The two main protagonists of the Battle of Bosworth. Henry Tudor left and Richard III on the right.

Step 6. Tudor History (1485 - 1603)

1485 King Henry VII 1485-1509

Henry Tudor, the first monarch of the House of Tudor. By marrying Elizabeth of York, daughter of Edward IV, he united the Houses of York and Lancaster. He was not popular, but everyone liked the Queen. He entertained huge numbers and his lavish living must surely have influenced his son, Henry VIII. His claim to the throne was very remote; he was Richard III's 5th cousin. After the death of Richard III, by marrying Elizabeth, no one was able to prevent Henry becoming King. However, having chosen Elizabeth of York as his queen, he was actually choosing the daughter of a king who himself had no right to the throne since he was illegitimate. (Is it any wonder he, with his family, went about blackening the name of his predecessor?)

He ignored Parliament, but still managed to collect a vast sum of money to give to his son when he died.

Henry had a Lord Chancellor and Archbishop of Canterbury called John Morton who developed a two-pronged argument that supported the raising of taxation; it was called Morton's Fork. The argument went thus: if you have an extravagant lifestyle, this proves you have enough money to pay the tax, whereas if you have a parsimonious one, this shows that you can also pay the tax because you have set enough money aside to do so.

Lambert Simnel and Perkin Warbeck – Two famous pretenders to the throne:

Lambert Simnel

Was crowned in Dublin as Edward VI in 1487.

He was defeated at Stoke Field (Notts) and became a servant of Henry VII but was later executed. His backers tried to pretend he was Clarence's son (encouraged by the boy's tutor, the priest Richard Simon).

Perkin Warbeck

He was hanged, drawn and quartered in 1499 for pretending to be Richard, Duke of York. In 1498, he had landed at St Michael's Mount and reached Taunton with a large force before Henry VII could stop him.

Great Tudor Explorers

In 1453, the overland trade route to the East was closed by the Turks. They captured Constantinople.

In 1498, Vasco da Gama (Portuguese) reached India by sailing around Africa.

In 1492, Christopher Columbus, an Italian, but paid by the Spanish King, reached America by sailing across the Atlantic Ocean. He initially thought he had reached India.

The Pope then announced that all newly discovered land found west of the Azores belonged to Spain, and to the east belonged to Portugal (hence Brazil being Portuguese).

John Cabot, from Venice, paid by Henry VII in 1497, crossed the Atlantic and reached Newfoundland. He was lost in his ship in 1498 on his second trip.

The Portuguese nation became famous for naval explorers, due to the influence of Prince Henry the Navigator.

In 1486, Bartholomew Diaz rounded the Cape of Good Hope (then called the Cape of Storms).

The Mohammedans, resenting this navigating success, attacked the Portuguese in 1509, at sea, but lost. After this, the Christian merchants controlled the seas.

Other English explorers included Gilbert and Frobisher, who visited Newfoundland and Labrador.

Sir Walter Raleigh (step-brother of Gilbert) founded Virginia, which he named after Queen Elizabeth.

Sir Richard Grenville also visited Virginia in 1585, but angered both the Indians and the Spaniards by capturing their galleons.

Virginia was not successfully colonised until 1607.

1492 Christopher Columbus

Columbus was born at Genoa in about 1453.

After the fall of Constantinople, the overland route to Asia was closed, and Genoa became much less important as a seaport.

Columbus approached the Spanish with his suggestion of finding a route to Asia by sailing west. The Spanish were fighting the Moors and were not free to accept the offer until after their victory in 1492.

Columbus sailed in 3 ships, Santa Maria, Pinta and Nina. In October 1492 he reached San Salvador.
He called the natives Indians, because he thought he had reached India. We now call the islands the West Indies.
In all, he crossed the Atlantic four times, but the Spanish regarded him as a failure because he never reached India.
Columbus was always supported by King Ferdinand and Queen Isabella.

Followers of Columbus
America was probably named after Amerigo Vespucci, the first man to declare that it was not Asia.
Because Cabral, a Portuguese, had landed in Brazil, it became the only country south of the USA to speak Portuguese – all the rest speak Spanish.
Magellan sailed south and around South America into the Pacific Ocean, so called because it was calm. The straits between the Continent and Tierra del Fuego are named after him.
While Magellan was killed in the Philippines, a small number of his sailors reached Portugal and thus became the first men to sail around the world..

Spain's Explorers
In 1513, the Spanish discovered the Pacific Ocean and Florida.
In 1519, Hernando Cortes discovered Mexico and the Aztecs, whose leader was called Montezuma.
Pizzaro discovered the Incas in Peru and their capital Cuzco.
Ferdinand de Soto explored the southern part of what is now the United States as far as the Mississippi and Coronado reached the Grand Canyon.
The explorers were always accompanied by missionary priests (mostly friars) and San Francisco began as a mission with a church, a school and a workshop.
It is due to these missionaries that Latin America became Catholic.
The Spanish did not exterminate the Indians, like the English did, in their colonies.

Elizabethan Sea Dogs

Sir John Hawkins made money from shipping slaves illegally from Africa to America. Sir Francis Drake was a pirate who captured ships and stole gold and silver. He was the first Englishman to sail around the world. Drake's ship was the Pelican, but he renamed it the Golden Hind. Drake and Hawkins were cousins.

1500 Gypsies arrive in Britain

For Gypsy (an English corruption of the word Egyptian) one should say Romany. They are nomadic people whose language is called Romany and who originated in North Western India.

1509 Henry VIII

He reigned from 1509-1547.

He was called Defender of the Faith by Pope Leo X for his paper defending the seven sacraments and criticising Luther.

He married his brother's widow, Catherine of Aragon, with the Pope's permission.

When she failed to produce a son, he, with no real cause, doubted whether his marriage to her was valid.

His six "wives" were: Catherine of Aragon – divorced
Anne Boleyn – beheaded
Jane Seymour – died
Anne of Cleaves – divorced
Catherine Howard – beheaded
Catherine Parr – survived.

Thomas Cardinal Wolsey failed to get the Pope to annual Henry's marriage to Catherine of Aragon and was sacked as Chancellor.

Wolsey was succeeded by Sir Thomas More, but More (later St Thomas More) was executed for refusing to accept Henry as head of the Church.

More was succeeded by Thomas Cromwell who was executed for arranging the marriage with Anne of Cleaves, and this in spite of his work "dissolving" the monasteries – see below.

Cromwell was succeeded by Archbishop Thomas Cranmer.

St James's Palace in London was built between 1531 and 1536.

St James's Palace in London

Before his fall, Henry's appearance was very impressive. He was tall, good looking, richly clothed and with a red beard. He would hear three Masses a day; he loved hunting, music and tennis. Later, he became obese and degenerate. For his family tree please see Appendix 4c.

The Court of Star Chamber

It was the room where the King and his council would meet.

It was called Star Chamber from the stars on the ceiling.

It began in the reign of Edward III.

It was the senior court of the land.

Henry VII used it to keep his nobles under control.

It was subject to its own rules, was unpopular, and Parliament abolished it in 1641.

In the reign of Henry VIII, Cardinal Wolsey made great use of the Court of Star Chamber, tending to treat his opponents badly.

1513 Battle of Flodden

Henry VII married his daughter Margaret to James IV of Scotland, in order to unite both countries.

But the English in the north kept on raiding the Scottish borders.

When Henry VIII went to war with France in 1513, James decided it was the best time to teach the northern English a lesson.

They marched from Edinburgh and stopped near Flodden with an army of over 30,000 men (some say up to 60,000).
The Earl of Surrey marched north with 25,000 men and placed his soldiers behind the Scots, cutting off their retreat.
In the battle, many Scots were killed, including King James IV of Scotland.

The site of Flodden Battlefield with kind permission of Clive Hallam-Baker©

1520 Field of Cloth of Gold

It was held in 1520 just south of Calais.
It was a grand "picnic" at which Henry VIII and Francis I made friends.
A temporary palace and 2,800 tents were erected.

Cricket

The first game of cricket appears to have been played in the 16th century, although there are reports of Cistercian Monks in Guildford having invented the game in the 13th century. They developed the game to illustrate the doctrine of the Holy Trinity, the bowler representing Satan.

16th Century Ireland

In 1541, and after the break with Rome (The Act of Supremacy in 1534), Henry VIII declared himself King of Ireland.
The Irish, remaining Catholic, resisted Henry's imposition.
Henry flooded Northern Ireland with English settlers, and in 1601 the Irish army was defeated at Kinsale.

However, the English could never get the Irish to give up their Catholic Faith.

Renaissance/Reformation

In Roman times, Constantine moved his capital city from Rome to Byzantium. He renamed it Constantinople and it became a splendid Catholic centre.

In 1453, when it fell to Islam, the Greek scholars fled to Italy where their influence began the Renaissance or "rebirth." The rebirth meant the rebirth of the culture of the Roman and Greek Empires, and some say it was the fulfilment of the Middle Ages. It was centred principally at Florence in Tuscany, where it was financed by wealthy families, particularly the Medici family.

While many of the works of art were religious, others were unquestionably immoral. Partly as result of their lewd nature, the renaissance led to a diminution of Christianity, which some thought to be less important than classical beliefs. As a result, Humanism and Liberalism began to spread.

The startling development in painting was the use of perspective. Modern research indicates that this may have been perfected by the use of the *Camera Obscura*.

The principle artists were:

The Bellini Brothers	Venice
Leonardo da Vinci	Florence and Milan
Raphael	Perugia and Florence
Michaelangelo	Florence and Rome
Titian	Venice
Tintoretto	Venice
Durer	Germany

1529 Cardinal Wolsey and Anne Boleyn

In 1529, Pope Clement VII ruled against Henry VIII getting an annulment of his marriage with Catherine of Aragon, Emperor Charles V's aunt, and daughter of Ferdinand and Isabella. Henry wanted to divorce Catherine and to marry Anne Boleyn (whom some, including Anne's mother, declared to be Henry's own illegitimate daughter). Henry promptly dismissed Cardinal Wolsey, his Chancellor, whom he saw as being responsible for his failure to procure an

annulment. He was on his way to London to stand trial when he died at Leicester in 1530.
In 1533, Henry married Anne.

Hampton Court
Wolsey was very powerful and immensely rich and it was he who built Hampton Court.

Hampton Court © Plus one / Shutterstock.com

On a visit to Hampton Court one can see:
- Kitchens
- Cellars
- Private Royal apartments
- Fountain Court
- Cardinal Wolsey's rooms with paintings of Tudors
- State apartments, Great Hall, Chapel
- Tennis Courts – Royal Tennis was invented in France
- Maze
- Royal Toys

The Protestant Reformation

This essentially began with Luther in Germany in 1512.

Luther attacked the Pope and the Catholic practice of granting indulgences.

Henry VIII began by opposing Luther and was given the title "Defender of the Faith" by the Pope for his resistance to Protestantism. However, when Clement VII refused to allow Henry to divorce, Henry assumed papal authority in England for himself and to this day British monarchs claim the title, "Defender of the Faith."

Once Henry had made himself the equivalent of the Pope, he decided he must have all the Church's land and property as well.

Thus the Reformation in England began, in part, with greed. Once the Church was no longer loyal to the Pope, other people began to change the religion as they pleased. Hence the many, fragmented variations of Protestantism.

1534 Act of Supremacy

In 1534, Parliament was forced by Henry, who threatened violence on members who did not co-operate, into passing the Act of Supremacy. This Act made Henry, who was neither priest nor in any respect trained as one, supreme head of the Church in England. As such he was given the right to exercise even greater spiritual power than had belonged to popes, apart from the powers of confecting and administering the sacraments. In 1535, Sir Thomas More, Henry's chancellor, was indeed executed for failing to support the King. More's acknowledgement of the supremacy of the Pope led to his martyrdom. "My Lord," the saint said at his trial "for one bishop of your opinion, I have a hundred saints of mine."

End of the Middle Ages

1534 is often recognised as being the year that marked the end of the Middle Ages and the start of the modern world (early modern era). It marked the end of papal supremacy in Great Britain.

1535 Saints Thomas More and John Fisher martyred.

In 1535, Thomas More and Archbishop John Fisher were beheaded in London for refusing to accept the Act of Supremacy. More had been Henry VIII's Chancellor.

St John Fisher

He was a Cardinal and Bishop of Rochester.
He opposed and resisted Henry VIII's divorce from Catherine of Aragon, for which he was tried for treason.
He was martyred on Tower Hill on 22nd June 1535 (the same year as St Thomas More). He too is a canonised saint.

Dissolution of the Monasteries

That same year the suppression (destruction) of the monasteries began. Once Henry had made himself "Pope", he could see that he was responsible for the religious lands and their vast assets. He thus sent visitors to the monasteries commanding them to snoop around and note down all their possessions.
Any monks who showed they were against the King's divorce were sent to the Tower or forced out of their monasteries.
The silver, gold and lands, etc., were all taken over by the King.
Cranmer became Archbishop of Canterbury, the first married Archbishop of Canterbury – and the first Protestant one; Cromwell became Chancellor.
Cromwell and Henry were quite ruthless. They executed any who opposed them, whether abbots, monks or lay people.
The smaller religious houses were closed and sold in 1536; the larger ones in 1539 (nearly 1,000 in all). The monks and servants were simply expelled. The lands and treasures, where they were not appropriated by the King, passed to those who had helped him.
What is often forgotten in this theft of the millennia is that, in virtually every case the assets belonged to the monasteries as a result of freely given donations. Nonetheless, they were, in part, taken by Henry for himself and, also in part, given to Henry's favourites.
And against this, the social and moral good the monasteries did through their hospitals, schools, road building and maintenance, hospitality for travellers and help for the poor, suddenly ceased, instigating an era of major poverty and hardship.

The remains of a "dissolved" abbey. This is Tavistock Abbey in Devon

Fountains Abbey in Yorkshire © Michael Warwick / Shutterstock.com

The Protestant religion

The new Protestant religion (which was called Protestant because it protested against papal authority) called for war against the Catholic Church throughout Europe, with the demand that all who refused to give up their faith should be put to the sword. In view of this threat, the Catholic Church decided to defend itself vigorously and this led to the "Counter-Reformation."

The long-term effect of the Reformation was the introduction of Protestant thinking. This was to divide the world into two separate political systems. Whereas before the Reformation, authority came from God and the Catholic Church, afterwards it came either from the state (eventually Socialism and Communism) or from one's personal beliefs, whatever they might be; and this adoption of personal authority has led to the development of both Capitalism and Rationalism. Since the Reformation there has been no single institution in Europe unifying it and supplying the people with ethical guidance, which it then enforces.

Book burning

One of the greatest tragedies (and there were many great tragedies) of the Reformation, was the systematic destruction by fire of the books of the old religion. The spiritual masterpieces, as well as the books of mediaeval history were piled high and set alight. The monastic libraries were obliterated and their other possessions either destroyed or given away to Henry VIII's favourites.

Stifling of the circulation of knowledge

Before the Reformation, abbots in England would meet every year to disseminate knowledge of scientific advances. It is generally reckoned that the Reformation delayed the Industrial Revolution by two and a half centuries. Indeed, in 1550, no degree of any kind was taken at Oxford University.

Enclosures

In the mid-16th century, the enclosure of common land in England (enclosing what had hitherto been enjoyed by the community, and denying access by the community to it) curtailed common grazing rights and caused wide-spread hardship.

Originally, enclosing land had begun in the 12th century. The land enclosed had been farmed systematically, mainly under monastic supervision, with the result that enclosed land tended to be most productive. After the Reformation, when so much land was handed to the favourites of Henry VIII, the new owners saw how much more productive, and therefore more profitable, the enclosed lands were and thus they tended to keep the poor, and their animals, from using such areas.

By the early 18th century, almost all common land had been enclosed, but the General Enclosure Acts of that time established procedures to safeguard tenant rights.

1536 Anne Boleyn beheaded

In 1536, Henry divorced Anne Boleyn and then had her executed. He declared her daughter Elizabeth illegitimate and had her barred from succeeding to the throne. He married Jane Seymour (followed by three subsequent wives). Henry himself died in 1547.

There are rumours that Anne Boleyn may have been Henry's own daughter. Apparently her mother, an old flame of Henry's, begged him not to enter into a relationship with Anne.
She was crowned in 1533, but executed in 1536.
It was Henry's lust for Anne that led to the Protestant Reformation in England.

Thomas Cromwell

He became friendly with Henry VIII by joining the enemies of Wolsey.
It was he who persuaded Henry to take the title of Supreme Head of the Church of England.
The dissolution of the monasteries was organised by him as part of his aim of abolishing papal authority.
He fell from his high office (chancellor) when Henry lost interest in Anne of Cleeves, whom Cromwell had chosen.
He was beheaded on Tower Hill in 1540.

Pilgrimage of Grace

It was led by Robert Aske in 1536, in opposition to Henry VIII's break with Rome and the dissolution of the monasteries.
The whole of Yorkshire rose in rebellion.
They took York, but when they reached London, Aske was arrested and executed.
A similar rebellion began in Devon and Cornwall, under Edward VI, called the Prayer Book Rebellion, in 1549 (demanding the restoration of the Latin Mass).
It too was crushed and thousands were killed.

1536-1543 Acts of Union between England and Wales

These united England and Wales, with Wales accepting Protestantism. Non-Conformity became firmly established in Wales in the 18th Century.

1540 John Knox Introduces Calvinism to Scotland

Calvinism is a major branch of Protestantism but, within its folds, there are many variations of belief

1545 Mary Rose (Henry VIII's Flagship) sunk.

This ship was raised in 1982 and the remains of the ship can be seen in Portsmouth.

View from the stern toward the bow of the conserved starboard side of the Mary Rose. Long galleries beside the ship on three levels display some of the 19,000 objects recovered opposite where they were found on the ship. ©Mary Rose Trust

1547 Edward VI

He reigned from 1547-1553, dying at the age of 15.
On his accession, and to enforce his father's claim to spiritual supremacy in England, at the age of nine he was declared, in effect, "pope" of England, with authority and power to legislate on all spiritual matters. This meant that…
During his reign the Protestant religion was further enforced by his uncle, Edward Seymour, Duke of Somerset (Protector Somerset).
Edward wished for the crown to be passed on his death to the Protestant Lady Jane Grey.
During his reign (1549) the Book of Common Prayer was produced by Archbishop Cranmer.
Somerset was Lord Protector of all England, but was sacked for supporting the suffering peasants and executed in 1552. His place was taken by the Duke of Northumberland.

1549 The Book of Common Prayer

In 1549, the Book of Common Prayer was introduced in English.
The Act of Uniformity made its use compulsory and abolished the Latin Mass.
It was written by Cranmer.
It led to the Prayer Book Rebellion in Devon and Cornwall in 1549.
In 1552, a revised version was printed.

1553 Queen Mary

In 1553, Mary reigned in England until her death five years later (succeeding her half-brother, Edward, who reigned from age 9-15 and was a Protestant, under the control of Protestant advisers). When she ascended the throne, Parliament and the people immediately, voluntarily and enthusiastically, re-embraced the Catholic faith. Indeed, her accession to the throne and procession through London to claim it, was probably the most popularly endorsed, seeing, proportionately, the largest crowds, in England's entire history.
When Mary came to the throne, Catholicism was immediately restored. No laws needed to be passed to achieve this, and it was enthusiastically re-endorsed by the English people.
The Protestants rose in rebellion against the plan for her to be married to Phillip II of Spain in 1554. They were led by Thomas Wyatt. The rebellion failed and…
she did indeed marry Philip, whose son by an earlier marriage was Don Carlos. Philip persuaded Mary to go to war with France, the result of which was that Calais, the last English possession in France, was lost in 1558.
Under Cardinal Pole's advice, the heretical bishops, Latimer and Ridley, were burned at the stake. They had been given every chance of escape but, like Archbishop Cranmer, their hatred of Catholicism was so great that they chose death over exile.
She is called "Bloody" because during her reign 287 Protestants were put to death. However, not only were such executions a part of every monarch's reign at the time (on average there were 12,000 executions every year and so these executions must be viewed in this context), all countries punished unrepented heresy by execution (usually burning), and some of its most enthusiastic proponents were Protestants, like Hugh Latimer. Mary herself was never in

favour of the executions; the decisions being forced on her by her advisers who themselves became Protestants in the next reign, that of Queen Elizabeth (who is far more deserving of the epithet "bloody" in her treatment of Catholics. In Elizabeth's reign simply being a Catholic priest was sufficient to be put to death).

Mary's chief religious adviser was, as we have seen (the in fact rather progressive) Cardinal Pole, who was the last Catholic Archbishop of Canterbury and who, with Mary's husband, Philip II of Spain, was against capital punishment for heresy, and who implemented the policies of the "Counter-Reformation" with great success, in such a short time, in England.

Lady Jane Grey

She was the great-niece of Henry VIII and a Protestant who, after the death of Edward VI, reigned for nine days in 1553.

She was planted on the throne by her father-in-law, the Duke of Northumberland, who had been Edward's main adviser.

She, her husband and Northumberland were all executed when the country rebelled in favour of the King's Catholic daughter Mary.

1556 Execution of Archbishop Cranmer

He was Archbishop of Canterbury under Henry VIII.

He was burned at the stake in 1556 under Mary.

Despite being given every chance of escape, he died an unrepentant Protestant, having confessed his heresy, and then recanted, numerous times, wherein no sincerity may be surmised.

1558 Queen Elizabeth

She reigned from 1558-1603.

She was the daughter of Anne Boleyn, and therefore quite possibly the product of incest because Anne Boleyn's mother had been one of Henry VIII's mistresses.

She outlawed the Catholic Faith, killing many Catholic priests and lay people.

Blessed Cuthbert Mayne was the first priest to die for the Faith in her reign (in

Launceston). Many of the Catholic martyrs were executed at Tyburn, near Marble Arch.

The plaque marking the site of Tyburn Tree, where many Catholic martyrs met their death. It is near Marble Arch in London

The plaque in Holywell Street Oxford marking the site of the Catholic martyrs of that city

It was during her reign that many of the priest holes were created – hidden spaces in houses in which a Catholic priest might hide to escape persecution and almost certain death. There are many priest holes that can still be seen – Ufton Court in Berkshire has two such niches.

Ufton Court near Reading in Berks©

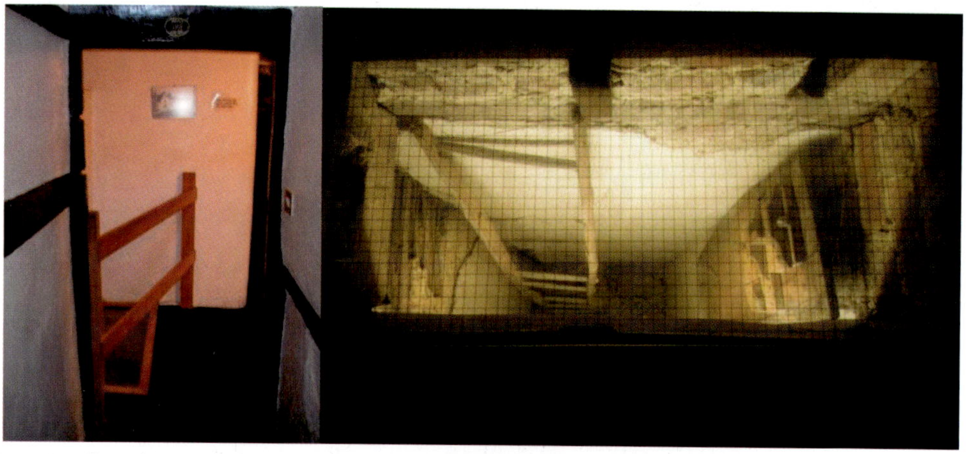

The siting © and interior © of one of the priest holes at Ufton Court – all three photographs with kind permission of the trustees of the Ufton Court Educational Trust

Relics from this time. The one on the left contains the relics of the first priest to be put to death in Elizabeth's reign, Blessed Cuthbert Mayne.

Elizabeth signed the death warrant of Mary Queen of Scots in 1587.
Her main adviser was William Cecil.
She fined all who refused to attend Protestant services (these people are called recusants).
Those who wanted the church to become even more Protestant were called Puritans.
Between 1598 and 1878 Rome appointed Vicars Apostolic to provide religious authority for Catholics in Britain, which was divided into regions for the purpose. They were not referred to as being bishops because that would have antagonised the Protestants. The most famous leader of British Catholics during this long period of persecution was Bishop Richard Challoner. During this time a number of religious foundations were established, usually in secret; arguably the most famous of these being the Bar Convent founded in York in 1686.

Mary Queen of Scots

She was born at the Palace of Linlithgo in Scotland in 1542 and was executed in 1587.

Linlithgo Palace © Roy Henderson / Shutterstock.com

When her father died, six days later she went with her mother, Mary of Guise, to live in France.

In 1558, having married the Dauphin, she became Queen of France.

When the King of France died in 1560, she returned to Scotland.

In 1565, she married Lord Darnley but their lives together were fraught with violence and death. One of the more gruesome examples being the murder of her servant Rizzio in the Palace of Holyrood House.

The Palace of Holyroodhouse.(c) Tan Art / Shutterstock.com

In 1567, Darnley was killed. Mary was suspected of being involved, mainly due to the existence of the eight so-called "Casket Letters," which appeared to show her complicity in the death of Darnley. Whether they were forgeries or not,

Mary, after a period of imprisonment and the Battle of Langside, she eventually fled to England.

Once in England, Elizabeth feared Mary's rightful claim to the throne (Europe said Elizabeth was illegitimate with no right to the throne, whereas Mary was effectively next in line). Mary was imprisoned and, after nineteen years, Elizabeth signed her death warrant. She was executed at Fotheringhay Castle. She never abandoned her Catholic faith.

During her imprisonment there were a number of attempts to free her (some may have been invented by her enemies). Chief amongst these was the Northern Rising in 1569 which, as its name implies, arose in the north of England but was ruthlessly suppressed. There were also plots to free her, the most significant of which, whether genuine or not, were the Babington Plot of 1568, the Ridolfi Plot of 1571 and the Throckmorton Plot of 1583.

1568 Babington Plot

The circumstances surrounding this failed plot, like the Throckmorton plot three years before, to rescue Mary Queen of Scots are disputed. Some say that it was incompetently organised, others that it never existed, but was fabricated by Elizabeth I's Secretary of State, Sir Francis Walsingham, and other enemies of Mary, to facilitate her execution the following year.

1586 Execution of Mary Queen of Scots

In February, 1587, after 18 years of being held prisoner by Queen Elizabeth I, Mary Queen of Scots was unjustly executed (some say "judicially murdered") at Fotheringhay Castle on a trumped up charge of treason against her cousin Queen Elizabeth. (For photograph of all that remains of Fotheringhay Castle please refer back to 1483.)

1588 Spanish Armada

Outraged by the news of Mary's execution, as well as the unprovoked attack by the English seafarer Sir Francis Drake on Spanish lands and shipping, in the summer of 1588, Philip sent the Spanish Armada, under the command of the Duke of Medina Sidonia, to the Netherlands to pick up troops for an invasion of England and to restore Catholicism to Britain. This ended in disaster and great

suffering for the Spanish, whose galleons that could, fled around Scotland, but more than 10,000 Spaniards lost their lives. In 1587 Drake had delayed the Armada by sailing into Cadiz harbour and attacking Spanish ships – an action known as "Singeing the King of Spain's Beard"
The punishment was mainly inflicted by the English fleet under Drake who had gained his maritime skills as a pirate or privateer in the West Indies, attacking Spanish treasure ships. (In the following century, such quasi-legal pirates were known as buccaneers.)

The view from Plymouth Hoe where Drake was reputedly playing bowls when he first sighted the Spanish Armada.

A little known fact is that in the following year, Drake sailed to Spain with an English Armada with the aim of destroying the Spanish fleet but he and it were utterly humiliated by the victorious Spanish forces who rubbed salt into the wound in 1589 when they invaded Mount's Bay, in Cornwall, and severely damaged the town of Penzance.

1591 Ireland defeats the English

In Ireland, the Catholics under the O'Neills and the O'Donnells defeated the English by 1600, and controlled the island again. At that time, Ulster was particularly anti-English.
Early in the seventeenth century, James I, who had given the Irish the right to practice their religion, attacked Ireland again and began to colonise Ulster with Protestants, mainly from Scotland (the Plantation of Ulster). This was to sow the seed for the troubles that would persist in later centuries and particularly throughout the twentieth century.

1601 The Charities Act (The Poor Laws)

The legal definition of a charity dates back to this Statute of Elizabeth I, of 1601. Prior to this date there were few, if any, charities in existence because, as we have seen, everybody's needs, including those of the sick and poor, were looked after in Catholic England by the extensive network of monasteries. There was a legal requirement that 1/3 of a monastery's income belonged to the poor and needy and, with a monastery or priory of some religious order approximately every three miles in England, this law ensured that everybody's needs were attended to from the cradle to the grave.

The situation has been described very succinctly by Professor Thomas E. Woods who stated, "The Catholic Church invented charity as we know it in the West." After the Reformation, however, which involved the sudden destruction of the monasteries and the gradual disappearance of the guilds, which also operated under the same Catholic umbrella, the assets, which had been used to alleviate the needs of the poor, etc., including a vast acreage of land and extremely valuable treasures, were taken by Henry VIII who shared his plunder with his equally unscrupulous and greedy supporters. As a result, with no-one looking after the poor and needy, the nation's poverty and misery increased alarmingly. To begin with, the situation was made even worse by the passing of laws against vagrants and begging, but, within a few years, the situation became so desperate that even the rapacious rulers could no longer ignore it. As a result, during the second half of the sixteenth century, a publicly funded system developed whereby taxes paid by the developing middle classes began to alleviate the nation's suffering masses. We now call this system the Welfare State.

Where the State failed to meet a particular need, well-meaning individuals began to set up their own benevolent institutions to fill the gaps. These institutions needed a legal framework within which to operate and thus we get the Charities Act of 1601.

Step 7. The House of Stuart (1603 - 1714)

1603 King James I

He reigned from 1603-1625. His Catholic mother may not have been acceptable as Queen, but he, as a Protestant, was acceptable as King. It is interesting to note that Elizabeth I died childless whereas Mary Queen of Scots, through her son James, is the ancestor of all subsequent British monarchs.
It was under James I & VI that the crowns of England and Scotland were united.
He believed in the divine right of kings, which meant he would hardly listen to his Parliament. He has been called the "Wisest Fool in Christendom", being a fine scholar who summoned Parliament as much as Elizabeth had.
His intimate friend, George Villiers, Duke of Buckingham, was given power and money by James.
The most notable event in his reign was the Gunpowder Plot in 1605.
The "King James Bible" was published in 1611. To some extent this was based on the first English version of the Bible that William Tyndale had published in 1494.
James' first cousin, Arabella Stuart, was favoured by some to become monarch instead of James.

1605 Gunpowder Plot

When James I became King, Catholics hoped that, in memory of his mother, Mary Queen of Scots, James would give back their freedoms. When he refused, the story goes that a group of Catholics led by Robert Catesby, resolved to blow up King, Lords and Commons, in the 1605 State Opening of Parliament.
The plan, it is claimed, had been that with the King dead, English Catholics would appeal for help to Spain and put Princess Elizabeth (James's daughter) on the throne. But one of the group lost his nerve and warned the Council of the supposed plot (the Monteagle letter). The Houses of Parliament were searched, the gunpowder discovered and the culprits arrested and executed.
The result of the Gunpowder Plot was an increase in hatred towards Catholics. There is significant evidence that the plot, or parts of it, was a deliberate hoax, designed to discredit Catholics and justify their persecution.

1610 Tea and Coffee

This was the year tea was introduced into Europe by the Dutch. Coffee drinking had begun in Arab countries in the fourteenth century, and coffee houses were opened throughout Europe in the 17th century. (See 1869 for reference to the tea clipper Cutty Sark.)

1615 Harrow School

Harrow took its first pupils in 1615.

Harrow School © Jennyt / Shutterstock.com

1616 Shakespeare dies.

William Shakespeare, England's greatest dramatist and poet, was born in 1564 in Stratford-upon-Avon and married Anne Hathaway. Having said that he died in 1616, this generally accepted fact introduces just one of the mysteries about him. Some claim that many of his plays were written years after this date. Other mysteries include the apparent code on his monument in Westminster Abbey and the exact nature of his relationship with Francis Bacon. There is also evidence to suggest that he was a Catholic (and that this is discernible in his plays as well).

Anne Hathaway's Cottage at Stratford-upon-Avon

Players acting parts of a Shakespeare play outside his old home in Stratford upon Avon.

17th Century

Metaphysical Poetry

The seventeenth century saw the birth of metaphysical poetry which involves concise verse that uses striking imagery. The foremost metaphysical poet is usually considered to be the Anglican clergyman, John Donne.

Parliament & King

Henry VIII had worked closely with Parliament, forcing it to agree with his proposals. This actually made Parliament more important after he died.
This importance increased as the monarch needed to ask more and more for money.
Eventually in Charles I's reign, he had such determination to act as he wished (exercising "the divine right of kings") that between 1629 and 1640, although he never held that he was above the law, he ruled without Parliament – the Eleven Years Tyranny.
After the Civil War, the King simply could not rule because he had no money to do so without Parliamentary approval. As a result, from then on Parliament became the governing authority.

Tunnage & Poundage

When James I came to the throne, Parliament voted him the customs duties (tunnage and poundage) for his income. Once they belonged to James, he thought he could increase them, but Parliament refused. However, the judges, whom James had appointed to settle the issue, agreed with James and so James dismissed his Parliament in 1611. The next Parliament (1614) was dismissed almost as soon as it had met and was called the Addled Parliament.

George Villiers, Duke of Buckingham
He was an intimate friend ("favourite") of King James I. James thought so highly of him that he gave to him, rather than to Parliament, the job of running the country between 1617 and 1628. He was unpopular and murdered at Portsmouth in 1628 by a man called Felton.

1618 Death of Sir Walter Raleigh
He was born in Devon in 1554. He is supposed to have laid his cloak over a puddle so that Queen Elizabeth I did not get her feet wet. His half-brother was Sir Humphrey Gilbert and his cousin Sir Richard Grenville.
He led an expedition to what is now North Carolina and brought tobacco to England and potatoes to Ireland.
He organised the defence of Devon against the Spanish Armada.
When James I came to the throne, Raleigh was unpopular and after an unfair trial he was imprisoned and beheaded in 1618.

The Thirty Years War
This was fought between Austria and its allies (Catholic) and Germany (Protestant) and was triggered by Protestants in Prague refusing to be governed by the Catholic Holy Roman Empire. In addition James I's daughter was driven out of Germany and the English wanted to declare war against the Catholic powers. James did not want war and forbade Parliament to discuss it.
When Catholic Spain refused to allow Charles to marry their King's daughter, Parliament was so indignant that war was declared on Spain. The war lasted from 1618-1648. The main result of the Thirty Years War was the devastation it wrought on the whole of Germany.

1620 Voyage of the Mayflower
The "Pilgrim Fathers" were Puritans, (extreme Protestants) who sailed to America in 1620 to be free to practice their religion. They sailed from

Plymouth, but some of their number came from Holland. They landed at Plymouth Rock, Massachusetts, and called their colony New England.
New York's first name was New Amsterdam, but it was later renamed New York in honour of James, Duke of York, who was to become King James II.
The journey to America was very rough.

Mayflower Steps in Plymouth, Devon

First Newspapers in Britain

The first titled newspaper, *Corante,* appeared in Britain in 1620.

1625 Charles I

He reigned from 1625-1649. He married Henrietta Maria, a Catholic.
He perpetuated his father, James I's belief in the divine right of kings; a belief that led to the English Civil War and his execution.
For eleven years (1629-1640) he ruled without Parliament. He appointed William Laud, Archbishop of Canterbury, a tough "high church" Anglican. Vicars who refused to obey Laud were tried by the Court of High Commission, lay-people by the Court of Star Chamber.

Sir Thomas Wentworth, Earl of Strafford

He was an adviser to Charles I. Strafford opposed Parliament, which passed an Act of Attainder, calling for his death without any trial. Charles, in fear of the mob, gave way and signed the Act and so Strafford was beheaded.

1628 The Petition of Right

The Petition of Right was drawn up in 1628 declaring that it was illegal to raise taxes without consent of Parliament and to imprison people without trial.

Charles I agreed to this.

1637 Ship Money

Ship Money was a tax the King could legally raise in time of danger. A port could either pay money or supply a ship to defend the land. In 1637, John Hampden refused to pay Ship Money because Parliament had not approved it. He was tried in court, but lost his case.

1638 Covenanters

In 1638, Archbishop Laud tried to impose the English Prayer Book on Scotland. The Scots rebelled, signed a covenant (hence covenanters) and Charles's army signed the peace treaty of Berwick without fighting a battle. The Scots complained that the Prayer Book was not Protestant enough.

1640 The Short Parliament

In 1640, Charles summoned Parliament to raise money for an army. The Commons refused to support the King until their own grievances had been remedied. The King refused, and dissolved Parliament.

The Long Parliament

This met in November 1640.
It was led by John Pym.
It:
- (i) organised Strafford's execution
- (ii) abolished the Court of Star Chamber
- (iii) abolished the Court of High Commission
- (iv) abolished Ship Money
- (v) said Parliament must meet every three years (the Triennial Bill)

Its members also included John Hampden and Oliver Cromwell.
Those who wanted to reform the Church of England were Roundheads, those who did not, Cavaliers.
When the Irish Catholics rebelled, Parliament needed an army. If the army had Charles's support, Parliament feared he would use it to attack them, so Pym drew up the Grand Remonstrance, attacking the King and removing his powers. This was passed and Parliament summoned its own army.

Charles reacted by marching on Parliament with 400 soldiers to arrest the five leaders – Hampden, Holles, Haselrig, Pym and Strode.
But they had escaped before Charles arrived. He is quoted as saying, "I see the birds have flown."
Charles went to York and both he and Parliament began to raise their armies for the Civil War.
Parliament appointed the Earl of Essex as General and ordered the Earl of Warwick to seize the navy.
In the Self-denying Ordinance, Parliament decided that no member of either house might take military command.

1641 The Grand Remonstrance

In November 1641, Parliament passed the Grand Remonstrance, which was a list of supposed acts of misrule by Charles I and which condemned the King's ecclesiastical policies. The leader of the House, John Pym, stirred up fervent anti-Catholicism.

1642 The Battle of Edgehill

Charles I raised his army at Nottingham in 1642.
One of his main officers was Prince Rupert of the Rhine.
They met the Parliamentary Army at Edgehill in October 1642 and routed it.
This gave the King Oxford, which became his headquarters.

It seems that it is not possible to visit the actual site of the Battle of Edgehill but one can enjoy a view of the site looking down from the village of Edgehill at the top of the ridge that gives this battle its name.

During 1643, most of the battles went the King's way.

1644 The Battle of Marston Moor

In early 1644, the Scots marched south and, together with the Parliamentary Army, besieged the King's forces in York.

Prince Rupert marched north and arrived at Marston Moor. The siege was instantly lifted.

Sir Thomas Fairfax charged the Royalist Army. To begin with the Roundheads did badly, but Oliver Cromwell regrouped his forces and attacked the Cavaliers from behind.

It became the Roundheads' first major victory.

However, it did not dishearten the Cavaliers who won further victories, especially at Lostwithiel. These caused the reorganisation of the Roundheads into the New Model Army under Sir Thomas Fairfax and Oliver Cromwell.

Monument marking the Battle of Marston Moor. © Northallertonman / Shutterstock.com

Civil War (Generally)

Not everyone fought in the war but nearly everyone suffered.

The soldiers were badly paid.

Houses were often looted.

There was much anti-Catholic propaganda.

1645 Civil War Ends

The New Model Army turned the whole war by winning the Battle of Naseby (1645).

The site of the battle of Naseby

Nine months later, the King surrendered at Oxford (1646) and the war was over. The King was taken from Holmby House in Northamptonshire to Hampton Court Palace by Cornet Joyce, but in 1647 he escaped to the Isle of Wight where he hoped to find refuge. His hopes were dashed when, instead of being welcomed on arrival, he was imprisoned in Carisbrooke Castle.

Carisbrooke Castle, Isle of Wight.

Courtesy of James Lancaster / CastlesFortsBattles.co.uk. Copyright Reserved

Many people rallied to the King's cause, including the Scots. The Scots were defeated at Preston (1648) and Cromwell also subdued the English Royalists throughout the south of England and Wales.
This ended the Second Civil War and Oliver Cromwell began the moves that were to lead to the execution of King Charles.
What was left of Parliament imposed heavy fines on all who had supported the King.

Oliver Cromwell

After the Civil War, Parliament refused the soldiers their back-pay.
Cromwell, who had been a very successful general in the Civil War, saw his chance and supported the soldiers.
The Army marched on London, forced eleven members of Parliament to leave, and offered terms to the King.
The terms were that everyone, except Catholics, might worship freely and the King must share power with Parliament. The King refused.
The King's refusal led to the brief Second Civil War in 1648. Once Cromwell had won this war, he decided the King must die.
This made Cromwell hated and he was never able to rule without force.

1648 Pride's Purge

Colonel Sir Thomas Pride expelled those Royalist members of Parliament who tried to negotiate a settlement with the defeated Charles I. The minority of members who were left constituted the Rump Parliament.

1649 Death of Charles I

After the arrest of the King, Parliament still had a majority that would never consent to the King's death.
Cromwell sent Colonel Pride with a force of soldiers to Parliament to arrest 50 members and bar entry to nearly 100 more (Pride's Purge).
The members left behind became known as the "Rump Parliament."
The King was then tried, but he refused to plead, because he said they had no right to try him.

The King was sentenced and executed outside the Banqueting House in London on 30th January 1649.

The Banqueting House in Whitehall, London with grateful thanks to © Walklondon.com

The Commonwealth and the Protectorate

When the Commonwealth began in 1649 it was very unpopular. Both Scotland and Ireland claimed Charles II as their ruler.

Cromwell went to Ireland and suppressed the Royalists ruthlessly. He killed thousands at the sieges of Drogheda and Wexford.

Scotland crowned Charles II; Cromwell went north and defeated the Scots at Dunbar, taking Edinburgh in 1650.

The Scots regrouped, went south to invade England, but Cromwell caught them and defeated them at Worcester in 1651.

The Levellers, a party in Parliament, wanted to do away with rank. Cromwell was against this, and while Parliament was sitting he ordered his troops to pull the Speaker from his chair and lock the doors. The Rump Parliament was thus at an end and so Cromwell organised a Parliament called "Barebones," but this was soon dissolved and Cromwell became Lord Protector. The Protectorate lasted from 1653 to 1659.

Charles II hides in an oak tree

In June, 1649, Charles II, hoping to regain his crown, landed in Scotland, was defeated in battles at Dunbar and Worcester, and fled to France. On his flight he had to hide in the Royal Oak of Boscobel.

The present Royal Oak of Boscobel © Craig Thornber at www.thornber.net

1651 The First Dutch War

During the English Civil War, the Dutch had built up their trade.
However, Charles I and the Rump had built up the English Navy.
When, in 1651, Parliament declared that all ships should salute the English flag in the channel, the Dutch declared war, which they lost in 1654.
Cromwell then set about attacking Spanish shipping (because Spain was Catholic) and defeated the Spanish at the Battle of the Dunes, near Dunkirk, in 1658. Blake was Cromwell's naval leader.

Thomas Hobbes published The Leviathan

Hobbes was considered to be the first English Protestant philosopher and he favoured absolutist government. His book caused a sensation because it upset both Parliamentarians as well as Royalists.

1653 Barebones Parliament

This was a short-lived Parliament named after one of its leading figures "Praise God" Barebones, which resigned its powers to Cromwell and was dissolved. It is also sometimes referred to as the "Parliament of saints."

1658 Tumbledown Dick

Cromwell died in 1658 and his son Richard assumed the title of Lord Protector. However, the people, who resented the way that Puritanism was being established by force, were ready to welcome Charles II as King. Richard Cromwell, known as Tumbledown Dick, resigned in 1659.

1660 Restoration of the Monarchy

Charles II was formally invited to return by a group of men led by General Monck. Monck, later 1st Duke of Albemarle, had originally been a Royalist, but swore allegiance to the Parliamentary cause to fight the Irish under Cromwell. Charles was a Protestant and signed the Clarendon Code in 1661 which asserted the supremacy of the Church of England over the Catholic cause.
Charles's main political advisers were **C**lifford, **A**shley Cooper, **B**uckingham, **A**rlington and **L**auderdale – from which we get the term "Cabal."

Royal Society founded

This is the premier scientific society in Great Britain, and numbered Isaac Newton amongst its members. In 1857 it moved to Burlington House, on Piccadilly, in London.

Burlington House, Piccadilly, London

Science, Writing & Learning in Restoration England

Williams Harvey described the circulation of the blood.
Robert Boyle discovered Boyle's law for gases.

Isaac Newton laid down laws which explained the movement of stars.
Samuel Pepys, the diarist, was president of the Royal Society and Clerk of the Acts of the Navy.
John Milton wrote Paradise Lost in 1667; John Bunyan wrote Pilgrim's Progress in 1678.
With theatres being reopened, many new plays were staged.
Newspapers such as *The Tattler* and *Spectator* began.

Transatlantic Trade and Limited Companies

Records show that by this time great wealth was arriving in Europe from the colonies across the Atlantic, mainly thanks to the institution of slavery. This trade led to the first limited companies being formed. Lloyds Insurance also began in Mr Lloyd's coffee house in 1687 with the "Lloyd's List" beginning in 1696.

Lloyds Building, today © Chameleonseye / Shutterstock.com

Charles II

He reigned from 1660-1685.
After the unpopularity of the Commonwealth, he was a very welcome monarch.
During his reign the following events took place:

- the Book of Common Prayer was published (1662)
- the Plague*
- the Fire of London*
- defeat by the Dutch*

The country was short of money and Charles was financed by Louis XIV (the Sun King) in return for English army help.

He is known as the "Merry Monarch" and he died a Catholic.
He was invited to reign by "The Sealed Knot" – a secret royalist association – and before he left the European mainland he issued the Declaration of Breda which was a general pardon to those who had taken up arms against the king, his father. One of the chief participants in the restoration of the British Monarchy was George Monck.
Having been invited to reign, Charles II had much less power over Parliament than his father.
The three events that are asterisked above caused widespread discontent and Charles found it easier to run the country with a group that came to be called a Cabal rather than Parliament.

1661 Clarendon Code

These were laws passed in 1661, establishing the Anglican Church as the Church of England. Neither Clarendon nor Charles II agreed with them.
By the Code, all other religions were suppressed.

1664 Second Dutch War

England's rivalry with Holland over trade led to war breaking out again in 1664. It went badly for England and when peace seemed likely, all the naval ships retreated to Chatham in 1667. At this the Dutch sailed up the Medway, broke into the harbour, burned four battleships and towed away the flag ship, the Royal Charles. The sailors, having not been paid, made no effort to stop them.

1665 The Great Plague

The Great Plague (1665) was similar to the Black Death. It affected London the worst. It was brought by fleas on black rats and ended when brown rats drove them out. The Great Fire of London destroyed many plague infested houses.

1666 The Great Fire of London

It began on 2nd September 1666, in Pudding Lane, and lasted until 5th September. Catholics were falsely suspected of starting it. The Monument was built to commemorate the fire.

The Monument (for that is all it is called) near the Tower of London

St Paul's and many churches, as well as 10,000 houses, were destroyed. The houses were rebuilt in brick. Sir Christopher Wren rebuilt St Paul's and many city churches.

St Paul's Cathedral in London

It was after this fire that throughout England fire precautions began to develop.

1667 John Milton wrote Paradise lost

1672 Declaration of Indulgence

In 1672, this was issued by Charles thus setting aside the laws against Catholics and non-conformists. Charles did not dare help one side without the other.

After the Third Dutch War, which he had lost, Charles needed money and asked Parliament to convene to vote it for him. Parliament met and cancelled the Declaration. Instead they passed the Test Act which dismissed all Catholics in government service (this included James, Duke of York). In 1685, James II issued a Declaration of Indulgence and ordered it to be read out in all churches. Seven bishops refused and were arrested and tried, but found not guilty.

The Third Dutch War
Louis XIV wanted to extend France's borders to the Rhine. To do this he invaded the Spanish Netherlands in 1672, with English forces to help him.
The Dutch beat him by flooding the land and defeating the English Navy off the coast of Suffolk.

Whigs and Tories (Part 1) (Part 2 can be found under the history of the House of Hanover. 1721AD)
This century also saw the launching in England of the first two political parties: Whigs (Liberals) and Tories (Conservatives). However, party politics only became the established norm later in this century during the heated exchanges over whether James II, a Catholic, should be allowed to inherit the crown.
Those who supported the Catholic succession were called Tories, a name given to Irish outlaws who plundered English settlers in Ireland (the Tories adopted the name "Conservative" in the 1830s). The term Whig was an abbreviation for Whiggamore, the name given to anti-royalists who had marched on Edinburgh in 1648.
In the second half of Charles II's reign, Charles's heir was his Catholic brother James. This worried the country and it was proposed that Charles's illegitimate son, the Duke of Monmouth, should succeed.
Charles did not want this and, with bribes from Louis XIV, he kept Monmouth's supporters quiet.
Monmouth's supporters then rallied around the Earl of Shaftsbury and became known as Whigs. Thus Whigs were anti-Catholic.
The party that united around Charles was known as Tories, whose name, as we have just seen, came from a band of Irish brigands.

1678 The Popish Plot

This was a plot invented by Titus Oates. He gossiped that Catholics were plotting to murder Charles, put James on the throne, land a French army and massacre leading Protestants. From 1678, at least 15 innocent Catholics were executed on Oates's false accusations, and scores of others accused and persecuted.

John Bunyan wrote Pilgrim's Progress

1680 Exclusion Bill

This Bill, which was never passed by Parliament, would have prevented James II from becoming King (1680).

1682 The Rye House Plot

This was a Protestant plot to murder Charles as he returned from racing at Newmarket. Rye House is 20 miles (or so) north of London.
The plot was ruined in 1682 by a fire at Newmarket which caused the King to return home early.

1685 James II

He reigned from 1685-1688.
Having converted to Catholicism, he was the last Catholic King of England.
He was an accomplished naval officer.
On succeeding to the throne, he was faced with the invasion by his Protestant illegitimate nephew, the Duke of Monmouth.
He defeated this invasion at the Battle of Sedgemoor (1685).
After the battle, many Protestants were tried by Judge Jeffries who hanged so many that his trials were known as the Bloody Assizes.
James tried to run the country with his Catholic supporters and resisted seven Protestant bishops who opposed him,
It was this aspect of his monarchy that so infuriated a small group of influential Protestants that they invited James's son-in-law, William, to become King instead.

William of Orange landed at Torbay in 1688, whereupon James's supporters deserted him. James and his family had to flee the country. It was because he was a Catholic that James was deposed and it wasn't Parliament, but a group of Protestants, who arranged for William to become King. The end of James's reign is known as the "Glorious Revolution."

The monument in Brixham, Torbay, to commemorate the landing of William of Orange – the so-called Glorious Revolution.

1688 William and Mary

They reigned from 1688-1702.

Neither had first claim to the throne and, unlike monarchs, their only title was that they ruled by Act of Parliament.

James II's son, James, a Catholic, was the true heir, and to prevent him succeeding, Parliament passed the Act of Settlement (1701) forbidding any Catholic from becoming King.
James II's son was called the Old Pretender..
When James II died, Louis XIV recognised James, the son, as King James III of England. This so infuriated the Whigs that they supported William in his wish to go to war with France.
This war is called the War of the Spanish Succession and England's famous general was the Duke of Marlborough.
William died when his horse tripped over a mole hill, after which the English Catholics raised their glasses and toasted "the Gentleman in Black Velvet."

The Glorious Revolution
James II's first wife, Anne Hyde, who died, had been a Protestant. His daughter (Mary) had married William, Prince of Orange, and ruler of Holland. Both were Protestants.
His second wife, Mary of Modena, was a Catholic who bore him a son, James, his first, in 1688.
The Protestants feared this son, a Catholic, because he was heir to the throne. A scurrilous rumour was put about that he wasn't James's son, but had been smuggled into the palace in a warming pan.
Thus frightened, a small group of Protestants encouraged William and Mary to come and claim the throne.
When Louis XIV invaded Germany, William could see that Holland was under no threat and so he sailed, landing at Torbay in November 1688.
When William had landed with his Dutch army, James's supporters deserted him. James sent his wife, Mary of Modena, and son out of the country and soon followed himself. As he left he deliberately threw his royal seal into the River Thames.
William didn't really want to become King (he was already King of Holland), but he didn't want to be junior to his wife, who was to become Queen. He agreed to rule jointly with her.
Parliament restricted both the powers and the income of William and Mary, and thus Parliament became the true source of government. A law was passed (the

Triennial Act) which meant elections to the House of Commons had to take place every three years.

1689 The Battle of the Boyne

After James II had escaped to France, he resolved to regain the English throne with Irish help.

In 1689, he landed in Ireland with French troops. The Irish were delighted to help him and together they laid siege to Protestant Londonderry.

William landed in Ireland and defeated his father-in-law at the Battle of the Boyne in July 1690.

Following this, the whole of Ireland was conquered by the English and, in spite of promises to the contrary, all Catholics were treated with great harshness. They could neither sit in Parliament nor vote. They could not become soldiers, sailors or teachers, and they were not allowed to hold land on a large scale.

Battle of Beachy Head

The French, sailing in support of the exiled James II, inflicted a disastrous defeat on a joint British-Dutch fleet.

Beachy Head © Niepo / Shutterstock.com

1692 The Massacre of Glencoe

Although the Kings of England had been Kings of Scotland as well since 1603, the two countries were quite separate.

Therefore it was necessary for William to be recognised as King of Scotland as soon as possible.

Certain Scottish nobles vowed not to acknowledge William as King. Although they won the Battle of Killiecrankie (1689) their leader, Bonny Dundee, was killed and the movement died out.

The Pass of Killiecrankie © Claire Fraser Photography / Shutterstock.com

To ensure all Highland Chiefs were loyal to William, they were required to take an oath before New Year's Day 1692. The MacDonalds of Glencoe were accidentally a few days late taking the oath.

William ordered the Campbells to punish the MacDonalds. After arriving in Glencoe, and behaving very warmly towards the MacDonalds, the Campbells suddenly murdered 38 of them and drove them from their land.

Glencoe – Thanks to Alex Blatchford ©

Battle of Cap de La Hogue

The British defeated the French navy in this naval battle.

1693 Battle of Cape St Vincent

The French were again victorious over a British fleet at the first battle of Cape St Vincent. (For details of the second battle see History Note 192 – Napoleonic Wars.)

1694 Bank of England founded

The Bank of England © Claudio Divizia / Shutterstock.com

The Bank of England was founded as a private company by William of Orange's backers to finance the nation's affairs following the Glorious Revolution. It would later be used to finance the wars that England waged against France and thus the National Debt effectively began at this time and for this purpose. Nowadays, the National Debt is the sum the Government has to borrow to finance all its activities that are not paid for by tax revenue.

It began by lending £1.2 million at 8% interest to the government to pay for King William's war. The loan and the bank were meant to last for ten years only, but the bank and its debt are now 300 years old.

It is in Threadneedle Street in the City of London.

While the Bank of England remained privately owned until its subordination to the Treasury in 1931, and nationalisation in 1946, its tiers of ownership are somewhat convoluted and it is still, essentially, like the US Federal Reserve (which was founded in 1913), a private business run by bankers. The reason for this, we are told, is that, logically, a government cannot lend money to itself.

Gentleman in Black Velvet

William of Orange (William III) died in 1694 when his horse stumbled on a molehill – resulting in English Jacobites (supporters of James II and his heirs) toasting the "gentleman in black velvet."

1695 Window Tax

This was a tax levied on the number of windows in a house, which led to the bricking up of windows in old houses. It was abolished in 1851.

1700 The War of the Spanish Succession 1700-1711

This war was a continuation of the War of the League of Augsburg (1689-1697) which was King William's successful attempt to subdue Louis XIV and prevent him returning James II (Catholic) to the English throne.

In 1700, King Charles II of Spain died childless. He left all his empire to the grandson of Louis XIV, thus giving France considerable power and renewing the opportunity of restoring a Catholic king to England.

France eased her way into Holland, excluded England and Holland from Spanish trade, and recognised James II's son, James Edward, as King of England.

The war began in more earnest in 1702, and the Duke of Marlborough led the English forces. The first great English victory was at Blenheim in 1704.

The French needed to fight the Austrians because, since Charles II's death, the Archduke claimed the Spanish throne.

In order to worry the French (i.e. take their mind off attacking the Austrians) the English sent a fleet to the Mediterranean. This fleet took Gibraltar and Minorca.

Having beaten the French, Marlborough pushed them back into France defeating them three more times at:

Ramilles 1706
Oudinarde 1708
Malplaquet 1709.

Marlborough was given Blenheim Palace in Oxfordshire as a reward.

Blenheim Palace

A bust of The First Duke of Marlborough in Blenheim Palace.

Grinling Gibbons

Grinling Gibbons is famous for his carvings, particularly in wood. However Blenheim Palace is full of his work – this one is in marble.

Marble carving by Grinling Gibbons

Gibraltar

Famous British naval commanders during this war include Admiral Sir George Rooke who commanded the allied naval forces in the capture of Gibraltar in 1704, and the splendidly named Admiral Sir Cloudesley Shovell who served under him. Shovell lost his life when several of his ships struck rocks off the Isles of Scilly; 2,000 lives were lost in what is considered to be one of the greatest maritime disasters in British history.

As a result of the Treaty of Utrecht, 1713, Philip of Anjou became King of Spain, the Spanish Netherlands were given to Austria, and England, keeping Gibraltar and Minorca, was given Nova Scotia and Newfoundland, improved trading rights, and thus had become a world power.

The Rock of Gibraltar ©- Thanks to the Gibraltar Tourist Board – visitgibraltar.gi

1700 Darien Scheme

The Scots wanted to found their own colony on the Isthmus of Darien, which is effectively Panama.

The English were trading overseas, so why not the Scots?

The Spanish drove the Scots away from Darien in 1700, and the English, having no wish to upset Spain, refused to help the Scots. The Scots also suffered terribly from disease while they were on Darien with many of the settlers dying.

1701 Act of Settlement

When it looked as if William and Mary and Anne would all die without providing an heir to the throne, the Whigs (traders and financiers) wanted to ensure Catholic James II and his successors were not restored to the throne.

The Whigs were more powerful than the Tories because they controlled the Bank of England which was owed £1.2 million by the government.
Thus, in 1701, while the Whigs were not in government, they were powerful enough to pass the Act of Settlement giving the crown to the Protestant descendants of James I, known as the House of Hanover.

1702 Queen Anne

She reigned from 1702-1714. She had 14 children, but none lived beyond the age of 11.
Her great and intimate friend was Sarah Churchill, wife of the Duke of Marlborough.
During Anne's reign, the great worry was that the Jacobites (Supporters of the ousted King James II) would succeed in placing his son, a Catholic, on the throne when she died.. To prevent this outcome Parliament amended the Act of Settlement to pass the crown on Anne's death to Protestant Hanoverians. This action was directly connected with the War of the Spanish Succession, which dominated her reign (see 1700 above.)

1703 Buckingham Palace Built

Buckingham Palace in London

1705 Halley's Comet

This was the year Sir Edmund Halley identified a number of comets, including the one which returns every 76 years and is named after him. It was next to return in 1758. He also rediscovered how to predict eclipses, a skill that had been developed by the Greeks two thousand years before, but was lost.

Halleys Comet © Media Resources / Shutterstock.com

1707 Act of Union between England and Scotland

In 1707, the English and Scottish Parliaments were merged.

Scotland had long been at odds with England and, on the death of Queen Anne, threatened to make its own choice of kings.

England, fearing this possibility, agreed to surrender her trading monopoly and accepted 45 members and 16 peers.

No alteration was made to the Scottish legal system.

Thus began the United Kingdom of Great Britain.

Step 8. Hanoverian History (1714 – 1901)

1714 King George I

He reigned from 1714-1727. He was married to Sophia Dorothea whom he divorced and imprisoned for life – see also George II. He spoke no English, spent much time in his native Germany and left the business of government to a group of ministers called a Cabinet. The main politician of his reign was Sir Robert Walpole. The two main events of his reign were the Jacobite Rising of 1715 and the collapse of the South Sea Company (known as the South Sea Bubble – see below).

1715 Riot Act

In 1715 there was considerable unrest caused by the opposition in England to "German George." This led Parliament to pass the Riot Act giving magistrates increased powers. It was effectively another anti-Catholic measure.

The '15 Rebellion

In 1715, James, son of James II, landed in Britain to promote what Rome and a number of European countries regarded as his legitimate claim to the British throne. He lost the Battle of Sherriffmuir and retreated. His forces were called Jacobites and were led by the Earl of Mar, known as Bobbing John. After the rebellion, General Wade built a system of military roads with which to control Scotland.

A General Wade Road © John A Cameron / Shutterstock.com

This James is known by his enemies as "The Old Pretender." He had two sons, Charles (Bonnie Prince Charlie - by contrast, "The Young Pretender") and Henry who was a cardinal. After Charles' death, and for those who recognised the Jacobite cause, Henry became the only cardinal-king in history. Henry, whose grandfather, James II, had fled from England with the crown jewels, returned them.

There was another little known, but associated, uprising in 1719. This was also defeated and ended at the Battle of Glen Shiel on the West coast of Scotland. One of the defeated Scots was Rob Roy, who was badly injured in the battle. (see also 1727AD)

1717 Freemasonry established in London

Freemasonry, the secret society which by this time had developed a strong anti-Catholic stance, set up its first lodge in London in 1717. This lodge is considered to be the "Mother Grand Lodge," or the most senior in the world.

Freemason's Hall in London © Baloncici / Shutterstock.com

South Sea Bubble

In 1717, the South Sea Company took over the National Debt and was going to pay for this debt by successful trading in the South Seas. The dream of vast profits from the South Seas led others to set up other companies for such trading. Thousands of people flocked to buy shares and this rush pushed the price of shares up by 1,000 per cent. Eventually, confidence in future profits collapsed and the shares in the companies became worthless – the Bubble burst. A man of great financial ability was needed to put the country on its feet again and Robert Walpole (Whig) came to power in 1721 and stayed there for 21 years. Walpole had been one of the few to benefit from the South Sea Bubble.

1721 Sir Robert Walpole

He was effectively the first British Prime Minister. Until the reign of George I, who spoke no English, the monarch chaired cabinet meetings. (It was not until 1905 that the term "prime minister" was formally acknowledged.) Sir Robert lived at No. 10 Downing Street, his official residence.

His brother-in-law, Charles Townshend, better known as Turnip Townshend, is renowned for his encouragement of improved farming methods.

Jethro Tull

Another famous agricultural pioneer from this time was Jethro Tull who invented the seed drill. Tull died in 1741.

Political Parties

It was during the 18th Century that political parties began to "whip" their MPs to vote according to party diktats and not their own individual preferences. In the French National Assembly, the Conservatives sat on the right, the Liberals on the left, and this is the origin of right-wing and left-wing politics.

Whigs and Tories (ii) (Continued from 1672 in Step 7)

The Whig party began late in the seventeenth century and drew its support from men engaged in trade and finance. The Tories formed themselves in opposition to the Whigs and represented the landowners, the Church of England, and above all the House of Stuart (i.e. James III). The Whigs favoured the House of Hanover and their rise to power coincided with both the founding of the Bank of England as well as the return of the Jews to England. The Jews sided with the Whigs who opposed Catholic James III. The Whigs, under Robert Walpole, were all powerful in the first half of the eighteenth century.

1727 -1760 George II

He reigned from 1727-1760. His father, George I, separated him from his mother after she committed adultery, and later, after George II had married, George I separated him and his wife from their children. The main events of his reign were:

- a war with Spain known as the War of Jenkins' Ear (1739)
- the War of the Austrian Succession (1743-48) and the Treaty of Aix-La-Chapelle
- the Seven Years War (1756-1763)
- the '45 Rebellion and Bonny Prince Charlie
- the foundation of the Indian Empire and Black Hole of Calcutta
- the capture of Quebec and the conquest of Canada

This war-faring King was the last British King to lead his troops into battle (at Dettingen in 1743).

1738 John Wesley/Methodism

In 1738, Wesley, who was an Anglican, founded Methodism, which was an attempt at evangelical renewal/revival in the Church of England. The Anglicans forced them out of their churches to preach in the open air such as at Gwennap Pit in Cornwall, and from this a separate church was born.

Gwennap Pit © Ian Woolcock / Shutterstock.com

1739 The War of Jenkins' Ear

Ever since the Treaty of Utrecht (1713), the Spanish had attacked British ships in revenge for Britain's improved trading rights. When Captain Jenkins, in 1739, told the House of Commons that Spaniards had boarded his ship and cut off his ear, the members replied by declaring war on Spain.

It was a short and unsuccessful war, subsumed into the War of Austrian succession, ending in 1748.

1741 Frederick the Great and the War of the Austrian Succession

In Austria, the Habsburg Maria Theresa became Holy Roman Empress in 1740. In spite of signing the Pragmatic Sanction which offered support and security to her, her Protestant neighbours in Prussia, under Frederick the Great, annexed the Austrian province of Silesia. (Silesia is a region of central Europe, but mainly in Poland.) In the ensuing war, France and Spain sided with Prussia, and Britain supported Maria Theresa. Austria won the Battle of Dettingen against the French and Prussians in 1743, at which the combined British and Austrian forces were commanded by King George II – the last occasion when a British Monarch led his nation's forces into battle. In 1746, however, when the British went to her aid again, they were defeated by the French under Marshall Saxe at Fontenoy. The war lasted for seven years and, although Silesia was granted to Prussia at the Treaty of Aix la Chapelle, as a result of her ultimate victory, Maria made Austria a very powerful force in Europe.

Dettingen was also the last battle in which the Yeomen of the Guard fought. These now ceremonial guards were established by Henry VII in 1485 as the bodyguard of the British sovereign. They are not the same body as the Yeoman Warders who guard the Tower of London (Beefeaters) who wear blue and not red uniforms.

Yeomen of the Guard © Kiev Victor / Shutterstock.com

Yeomen Warder (Beefeater) who guard the Tower of London
© Thomas Owen Jenkins / Shutterstock.com

1745 Bonnie Prince Charlie and the 1745 Rising

Thirty years after his father's attempt to regain the crown for the Stuarts, Bonnie Prince Charlie, "The Young Pretender," decided to try again.

He landed at Glenfinnan (in west Scotland) and within a month had reached Edinburgh where he defeated the English at Prestonpans. After reaching Derby, by which time the Hanoverian King George II had packed his possessions and was ready to flee, Bonnie Prince Charlie, with victory in his grasp, was betrayed by General Murray, who persuaded the Highland chiefs that they should retreat.

The Glen Finnan Monument © Mango-two-friendly / Shutterstock.com

1746 Battle of Culloden

The English, under the Duke of Cumberland (son of George II), chased the retreating Bonnie Prince Charlie and defeated him at Culloden on 17 April 1746. The defeated Scots were treated with great cruelty and many were killed by "Butcher" Cumberland, but after an exciting pursuit, Bonnie Prince Charlie escaped to France. This rising ended all Jacobite hopes of both unseating the Protestant Hanoverian kings, as well as successfully pursuing their claim to the British throne – a claim widely recognised in Europe.

The Monument that marks the Battle of Culloden © Meunierd / Shutterstock.com

"God Save Our Gracious Queen (King)"

The crushing of the Jacobite rising also resulted in the National Anthem being written and sung, to a tune by composer John Bull, to encourage a show of patriotism in defiance of future attacks of this nature.

1748 Trooping the Colour

This annual parade began this year, to celebrate the monarch's official birthday. It takes place each year on Horse Guards Parade in London.

The Trooping of the Colour at Horse Guards Parade in London © Ufuk Sivri / Shutterstock.com

1751 Gin Act

Gin was being drunk in London to such an extent that the city was said to be addicted to it; indeed Hogarth's prints are now famous for depicting the horrors that ensued from excessive gin consumption. This Act imposed a heavy duty on the drink and decreed that only licensed dealers could sell it.

1752 Britain finally adopts the Gregorian Reformed New Style Calendar

In Britain, eleven days were removed from the calendar with September 2nd being followed by September 14th. This move was very unpopular with the public. Rioters in London shouted, "Give us back our eleven days." In addition to this change, and henceforth, the year in Britain began on 1st January, and not 25th March.

The UK tax year however continues to begin, not on 25th March, but twelve days later on 6th April. This is not only because the Treasury thought they might lose eleven days of income as a result of the change and extended the end of income tax year to compensate, but they exacerbated the confusion by wrongly believing that the year 1800 was a leap year, and thus added an extra day to the eleven. This is why the income tax year ends on 5th April, despite calls to change it to a more convenient date.

1753 British Museum was founded

The British Museum in London © Jennyt / Shutterstock.com

1756 - 1763 The Seven Years War (Generally)

This lasted from 1756-1763 and involved Britain, Prussia, Austria and France. In the previous war (the war of Austrian Succession), Austria had sided with Britain, but, Britain having failed to keep Silesia for Austria, this time Austria sided with France, and Britain fought with Prussia to protect both Hanoverian interests as well as British naval interests around the world.

In 1756, the French seized Minorca. Admiral Byng was sent to relieve the island but failed and was executed, whereupon the French novelist Voltaire observed that "In England, it is good from time to time to kill an admiral, to encourage the others." Hence the expression, "Pour encourager les autres."

British morale was very low and William Pitt (the Elder), also known as the Great Commoner, came to the rescue. Most of the fighting was led by Clive in India and Wolfe in Canada. The British were victorious and added huge new territories with which to trade.

The Seven Years War in India

The British, in their war with the French, wanted to rid India of French factories. India was a valuable trading area and, by attacking the French, Britain hoped to increase her own trading opportunities, both in India and the rest of the Far East. The British, under Robert Clive, defeated the French at Plassey in

1757 and thus, through the trading activities of the East India Company, controlled most of India, particularly Bombay, Bengal, Madras and Calcutta.

The Black Hole of Calcutta

This was an incident in the Seven Years War. In 1756, Calcutta, an English trading post, was attacked and taken by the Nawab of Bengal. The Nawab was on the side of the French. A group of over 150 Europeans were locked in a small guardroom overnight and by the next morning 43 had died. This became known as the Black Hole of Calcutta. Clive recaptured Calcutta in 1757.

The Seven Years War in Canada

The French had a colony in Canada, and General Wolfe was sent by William Pitt the elder to subdue it. The key to success lay in whoever controlled Quebec.

Wolfe decided to attack the French forces under Montcalm by first of all capturing the Heights of Abraham above Quebec.

Wolfe succeeded in this by a risky and daring expedition. He took Quebec in 1759, but died in the battle.

Although the expansion by force of British interests around the world led to the creation of the British Empire by the beginning of the nineteenth century, an empire on which "the sun never set", the famous essayist, Samuel Johnson, disparagingly referred to the rivalry between Britain and France at the time as "a fight among robbers" and he invariably supported the Negroes whenever they rebelled against the British Colonialists.

William Pitt the Elder

He opposed Sir Robert Walpole and came to power in 1756, successfully directing the Seven Years War. His sympathy for the French Revolution (1789) was his undoing.

The East India Company

In 1600, some London merchants set up this company to handle the trade of spices and silk in India.

They set up a factory in Bombay, and when Charles II married Catherine of Braganza, a Portuguese princess who owned Bombay, the British hold on India was strengthened considerably.

In 1757, the French, who also had factories in India, fought the British under Robert Clive. The British won the Battle of Plassey and thus gained the rich province of Bengal.

The East India Company administered most of India and was in charge of handling events such as the Indian Mutiny in 1857.

The company ceased to exist in 1873.

1759 Handel dies

George Frederick Handel, the famous musician and composer, who was born in Germany in 1685, became a British subject in 1726. He is strongly associated with the Baroque movement in music.

1760 -1820 King George III

He reigned from 1760-1820. He was the first George to be brought up speaking English and was urged to "be a king" by his tutor. He tried to regain some of the powers lost by his predecessors. He had the right to appoint ministers and lay down policy, but Parliament had to approve his actions. MPs who wished to hold office, such as Walpole, both Pitts, etc., had not only to catch the King's notice, but to ensure that their own policies were supported by enough MPs for them to be able to govern. He is famous for losing the American Colonies.

His second son, Frederick Duke of York, was Commander in Chief of the army and it is of him that the nursery rhyme "The Grand Old Duke of York" was written, concerning his tactics on the hill at Cassell, just south of Dunkirk.

His chief ministers were Lord North and William Pitt, the Younger.

One of Pitt the Younger's arch-rivals was the colourful Whig statesman, Charles James Fox. Fox was controversial because he supported the American colonists, was anti-slavery but in favour of both Catholic emancipation, and the French Revolution.

He was a member of Brooks's Club which still stands today in St James's street.

Brooks's Club

When George III became senile, his son, George IV ran the country as Regent.

1765 The Stamp Act and the American War of Independence

In 1765, the British Parliament passed the Stamp Act which made all legal documents in the North American colonies subject to a tax. British legal documents already had to be taxed.

The colonists refused to pay the stamp duty and burned the papers because they said the British Parliament could not make them pay tax without them returning any MPs to the British Parliament.

The Stamp Act was repealed in 1766, but Parliament passed another Act declaring its right to make laws for the colonies.

These two Acts made the American colonists so rebellious that they, in turn, led to the American War of Independence.

1768 Encyclopaedia Britannica

This was the date of its first publication in Scotland. Since 1929 it has been published in the USA.

Canaletto dies

This Italian painter from Venice, whose real name was Antonio Canal, is famous for his oil paintings of his home city, as well as of England. He was born in 1697.

1772 Advances in astronomy and map-making

The surveyor and Astronomer Royal, Nevill Maskelyne, together with the mathematician, Charles Hutton, estimated the mass of the Earth, Sun, Moon and planets by measuring the mass of Schiehallion, an iconic peak in Perthshire, Scotland. Hutton also invented contour lines on maps

Schiehallion © Christapper / Shutterstock.com

1773 The Boston Tea Party

The tax imposed on tea in 1773 was very unpopular in North America.

A large body of men, who resented paying tax on tea, disguised themselves as Red Indians and boarded three tea ships in Boston Harbour. They threw hundreds of smashed crates of tea into the sea and this protest is known as the Boston Tea Party.

1775 - 1776 The American War of Independence

The disgruntled Americans rebelled in 1775 and were supported by France and Spain (in 1783, Britain was forced to accept their independence).

There were 13 British colonies that rebelled.

The reasons for the war were as follows:

- The American colonists were 3,000 miles from Britain and did not like being ordered about by a Parliament in which they had no representation.
- The Seven Years War in America, while successful, had cost Britain dearly and she looked to the colonists for help in payment. The colonists did not like paying for this war.
- See notes above on Stamp Act (p 142) and Boston Tea Party (p 143).
- To counter the British, the colonists set up their own parliament and protested against British treatment. In return, Lord North sent even more troops to America.

The first shots were fired in 1775 at Lexington.

In 1776, Congress made its Declaration of Independence and appointed General George Washington its Commander in Chief.

Part of the British troops surrendered at Saratoga in 1777 and the rest at Yorktown in 1781.

At the Treaty of Paris in 1783, Britain accepted American Independence, but due to a brilliant victory by Admiral Rodney over the French just before the treaty, Britain retained most of her other gains. (The treaty is also known at the Treaty of Versailles.)

1776 Declaration of Independence

It was drawn up by Thomas Jefferson. It was based on Thomas (Tom) Paine's writings. It was signed on 4th July 1776. It stated that all men are created equal and that governments exist to guarantee life, liberty and the pursuit of happiness. 4th July is celebrated every year in the USA as Independence Day.

The Armed Neutrality

During the American War of Independence, not only did France and Spain support the Americans, but Russia, Denmark and Sweden formed an alliance to protect their shipping.

This alliance, the Armed Neutrality, was formed to prevent England attacking their ships as well as the French and Spanish ships.

Death of John Harrison

He was the English inventor of the chronometer, a time-keeping apparatus with compensating mechanisms that could work at sea, or in any climate. This made time-keeping at sea, and therefore measurement of longitude, much more accurate. His contribution towards safety at sea was greatly under-appreciated and at the time the Admiralty made it very difficult for him to be recognised and rewarded for his achievement.

1778 Emancipation of Catholics & The Gordon Riots

In 1778, the Catholic Relief Bill was passed repealing some of the more oppressive laws against Catholics. Priests could say Mass again and Catholics buy and sell property. As a result, feeling against Catholics grew, and shouts of "No Popery" were raised everywhere. This culminated in the Gordon Riots in London, led by Lord George Gordon in 1780. The mob ransacked areas of London, burning Catholic chapels and order was only restored by the aid of 10,000 troops. 500 of the mob were killed and 25 executed, but Gordon was freed.

1779 Murder of Captain Cook in Hawaii

James Cook, a navigator and cartographer from Whitby in Yorkshire, made three journeys around the World. On the first (1769-71) in the Endeavour he visited Tahiti, New Zealand and Australia, and saw the Transit of Venus (when Venus can be seen crossing the disc of the Sun); on the second (1772-75) he visited the South Pacific and on the third (1776-79) he visited the North Pacific, but was murdered after a quarrel in Hawaii.

1780 The Derby

This foremost flat race for horses was first run. It is named after the 12th Earl of Derby, one of the promoters. It is an annual event on Epsom Downs, near London.

1783 Death of Capability Brown

This famous British Landscape designer had been born in 1716.

Capability Brown's design at Blenheim Palace

The Hunterian Museum opens in Glasgow

This was the first museum to open in Scotland. It was founded by anatomist John Hunter.

The Hunterian Musuem in Glasgow © Uriel M Ulan / Shutterstock.com

1787 Mutiny on the Bounty

This took place at Tahiti. The crew of HMS Bounty mutinied, leaving Captain Bligh and 18 officers aboard a small boat without maps. However, Bligh sailed over 3,500 miles to safety and, at a later court martial, was exonerated of any mistreatment of his crew, which might have led to the mutiny.

Lord's Cricket ground

Thomas Lord opened his cricket ground at Dorset Square in London as the home of the Marylebone Cricket Club. It was moved in 1814 to its present site in St John's Wood. Since 1884, every cricket test series has seen one match played there. The Oval became a cricket ground in 1845.

The Pavilion at Lord's

Romanticism

This was a fundamental and some would say degenerate development in Western art, music and literature. It flourished at the end of the eighteenth century and throughout much of the nineteenth. It embraced a concern for the relationship between man and his environment, particularly exploring the emotions. Romantic poets included: Keats, Byron and Shelley. Authors: Walter Scott, Jane Austen, Goethe, Schiller and Victor Hugo. Composers: Beethoven, Paganini and Schubert. Painters from the Romantic period included: Turner, Constable, De la Croix and David Roberts.

Joseph Mallord William Turner, The Fighting Temeraire tugged to her last berth to be broken up, 1838 © The National Gallery, London. Turner Bequest, 1856

John Constable, The Hay Wain © The National Gallery, London. Presented by Henry Vaughan, 1886

1792 Death of Robert Adam

He was born in 1728 and, with John Nash, was the most influential British Architect of this period. Charlotte Square in Edinburgh is probably his most impressive creation, but he was also strongly influential in the design of the beautiful Georgian buildings in Bath.

The Royal Crescent in Bath. Thanks to Martha Williams.(c)

1793 - 1815 Napoleonic Wars

England had been at war with France since the time of the French Revolution (1793), when the Convention (in France) offered help to all nations that wanted to overthrow their kings.

This war was marked by four British naval victories: the Glorious First of June (1794), the Battles of Cape St Vincent and Camperdown (1797), and the Battle of the Nile, which is also known as the Battle of Aboukir Bay (1798). It was ended in 1802 at the Peace of Amiens. (For the first Battle of Cape St Vincent see above 1693.)

When Napoleon crowned himself Emperor in 1804, he had already invaded Hanover and this act caused Britain to declare war against France, especially as France was threatening to invade England from Boulogne.

Austria and Russia sided with Britain, but Napoleon defeated them both at Austerlitz in 1805.

Later that year, Napoleon's successes were checked by Nelson's famous victory at Trafalgar.

Napoleon, having defeated the Prussians at Jena in 1806, issued the Berlin Decrees, forbidding any country to trade with Britain. Britain stood alone as all her allies had been defeated. One reminder of these wars that can still be seen is Dartmoor Prison which was built to house French prisoners of war.

Dartmoor Prison, Princetown

Napoleon then made his own brother King of Spain, at which the Spanish rebelled and British troops went to Portugal to assist Spain.

Russia refused to carry out the Berlin Decrees, so Napoleon invaded Russia in 1812 and defeated them at Borodino. While the Russians retreated, they destroyed the crops as they went (scorched earth policy) and although Napoleon entered Moscow, the Russians soon burnt their city down and the French had to retreat, returning home with only 5% of their army alive.

Napoleon was defeated at Leipzig in 1813 and in 1814 he was exiled to Elba.

In 1815 he returned to France only to be defeated at Waterloo – after this he was banished to St Helena until he died in 1821.

Battle of the Glorious First of June

The British, under Richard, 1st Earl of Howe, defeated the French near Ushant at this first naval encounter of the Napoleonic Wars.

1795 Orange Order

This organisation began in Northern Ireland as a secret society based on Freemasonry. Its aim was to act as the backbone of Ulster's resistance to the Irish Home Rule movement, as well as to counteract Catholic influence in the province. To this day it articulates hard line Protestant Unionism.

1796 Robert Burns dies

This famous Scottish poet had been born in 1759.

1797 Kubla Khan

This was the year Samuel Taylor Coleridge wrote his famous poem, *Kubla Khan*. Kublai Khan was the grandson of Genghis Khan.

Naval Mutinies

It was also the year of the Spithead Mutiny. It was started by sailors protesting about pay and conditions, and was particularly dangerous because Britain was at war with France at the time. While other mutinies at this time did not end with the sailors' grievances being addressed, in this case the sailors could claim victory.

Edmund Burke dies

He was a great and influential British conservative political philosopher.

1799 Battle of the Nile

In 1799, Admiral Nelson destroyed the French Fleet at the Battle of the Nile, forcing Napoleon to return to France.

Income Tax first levied

In 1799, Income Tax was levied in England to pay for the war against Napoleon.

1800 Britain and Ireland united

The Act of Union between these countries was passed in 1800. As part of this process, William Pitt the Younger, the British Prime Minister, used bribery to persuade the Irish Parliament to vote itself out of existence. The Union lasted until 1921.

Union Jack

The Union was marked, in 1801, by a redesign of the Union Jack (or, more properly, Union Flag) which had first appeared in 1603. This design is the same as the one in use today. The central red cross is the English Cross of St George, the white diagonal cross on a blue background represents the Scottish Cross of St Andrew and the red diagonal cross, the Cross of St Patrick.

1801 Thomas Paine dies

Paine, who was born British, but became an American political writer, encouraged both the American and French Revolutions. He wrote *The Rights of Man* and *The Age of Reason*.

1802 First British Elections

This was the year in which the first parliamentary elections to the House of Commons of the new united Parliament of Great Britain and Ireland were held, although voting was severely restricted. It would not be until 1929 that universal suffrage was granted to all men and women over the age of 21.

1805 Battle of Trafalgar

In 1805, the French, being unable to launch an invasion of England, left the Northern French ports for the Mediterranean. Admiral Horatio Nelson caught up with them on 21st October, off Cape Trafalgar, South-West Spain, and comprehensively beat them, thus ending French sea power and ensuring British naval supremacy in the English Channel. Nelson died in the battle but his flagship, HMS Victory, can still be visited in Portsmouth.

HMS Victory in Portsmouth

HMS Victory in Portsmouth

Martello Towers

These round towers (74 of them) were built on the south coast of Britain from Beachy Head to Folkestone as part of the defences against the threat from Napoleon. The name comes from Martello in Corsica where the French had built something very similar which had been very effective against British Bombardment.

A Martello Tower © Sally Wallis / Shutterstock.com

"Roll up that Map"

By 1805, Napoleon controlled so much of Europe after Austerlitz, and his power was so firmly entrenched, that the British Prime Minister, William Pitt the Younger, said "Roll up that map (of Europe) – we will not need it for the next ten years."

1806 The Berlin Decrees

Napoleon now issued the Berlin Decrees of 1806, forbidding any country that he had subdued from trading with Britain. This continental blockade was not only ineffective but resulted in Britain successfully being able to blockade all of France's territories.

1807 Slavery

The transport of slaves, which had made vast fortunes for those who arranged this extremely cruel treatment of their fellow human beings, was abolished in the British West Indies, principally as a result of the efforts of William Wilberforce MP. The ownership of slaves was not to become illegal in the British Empire until 1833.

1808 - 1814 The Peninsular War

This lasted from 1808-1814, when Napoleon placed his brother on the Spanish throne and the Spanish rebelled.

Britain decided to send troops to Lisbon and to attack the French from there. Due to the incompetence of two elderly generals, the British were forced to retreat to Corunna in 1809 and escape by sea (Sir John Moore's retreat).

Later in 1809, the British landed again, under Arthur Wellesley, (later created Duke of Wellington). The British had the following advantages:

I. Favourable geography
II. Command of the sea
III. Spanish guerrillas
IV. Wellington's ability

Wellington advanced into Spain, defeated the French at Talavera, but was unable to remain safely in Spain and retreated to Lisbon building the defensive fortification lines of Torres Vedras behind him.

Wellington's first victories came at Badajoz, Cuidad Rodrigo and Salamanca which enabled him to enter Madrid in 1812.

In the same year, Napoleon found himself in difficulties in Moscow and so, from Madrid, Wellington pushed north and defeated the French, first at Vittoria and finally in France at Toulouse.

1810 Highland Clearances

When owners of land in Scotland decided to try to improve it by introducing sheep, they cruelly evicted those who had previously been farming the land. This barbaric process led to mass emigration to Australia and North America, but with no improvement to the land. The clearances were also heavily directed at the Catholic population.

The depressing evidence of the Highland Clearances can still be seen throughout the Highlands of Scotland. © Peter Asprey /Shutterstock.com

1811 Luddites

Named after Ned Ludd, who smashed a textile machine in Leicestershire because it threatened his livelihood, these rioters were active between 1811 and 1816 and put the handloom operators out of work.

The dominance of the famous Lancashire Textile Mills, which flourished during this century, ended after World War I when British-financed mills were built in India.

A Textile Mill © Mirrormere / Shutterstock.com

1812 Napoleon's retreat from Moscow

Napoleon's march on Moscow in 1812 was a disaster. Although the French took Moscow and won the Battle of Borodino, they had to withdraw in bitter winter weather and the remains of the army were utterly defeated at Leipzig (The Battle of the Nations) in 1813. In 1814 Napoleon was sent into exile in Elba.

Assassination of Spencer Perceval

He was Prime Minister from 1809 to 1812, when he was assassinated by John Bellingham in the lobby of the House of Commons.

1815 Congress of Vienna

The French Empire was re-distributed at the Congress of Vienna (at which all the powers formed a "Holy Alliance" which even France was eventually to join). However, in February 1815, Napoleon escaped from Elba.

The Hundred Days

Napoleon entered Paris amidst wild acclaim and thus began his hundred days.

Battle of Waterloo

Wellington and Blucher, who, at the age of 73, still commanded the Prussian forces, were near the French in Brussels, but separated by 14 miles. Napoleon held Blucher at Ligny and without Wellington's help because the latter was

diverted by a (successful) encounter with the French at Quatre Bras. Two days later the rest of the French army then faced the British forces under Wellington at Waterloo (17th June.)
Napoleon was aided by his loyal colleague from his previous campaigns, Marshal Michel Ney, whom Napoleon called "the Bravest of the Brave." (Ney had been sent to arrest Napoleon but decided to join him instead.) Wellington defeated Napoleon in a very closely fought battle at Waterloo, but if General Blucher had not appeared when Napoleon had all but won, it is generally regarded that the outcome might have been different. Wellington not only never lost a battle; he never lost a single gun. Napoleon was sent into exile on the Atlantic island of St Helena where he died in 1821.

The Lion's Mound at the site of the Battle of Waterloo near Brussels in Belgium.
© Hans Engbers / Shutterstock.com

The Duke of Wellington
He lived from 1769-1852. He is most famous for leading the victorious British Armies during the Peninsular War (1808-1814) and at Waterloo in 1815. He was Prime Minister from 1828-1830, favoured Catholic Emancipation, but opposed electoral reform. He is known as the Iron Duke and is Britain's best known soldier. He is reputed to have said that the Battle of Waterloo was won on the playing fields of Eton. When Queen Victoria asked him how to get rid of the small birds that lived in the Great Exhibition building, he replied "Sparrow hawks, Ma'am."

Ghurkhas

Since 1815, Nepalese soldiers, called Ghurkhas, have been recruited to the British Army

The Gurkha Memorial in London

End of Impressment

It was about this time that the Royal Navy stopped forcing men violently to serve on its ships by means of their Press Gangs. This infamous practice had started at the end of the seventeenth century.

1816 Elgin Marbles arrive in England

This collection of ancient Greek sculptures, taken from the Parthenon in Athens, was saved from destruction at the hands of the occupying Turks by the Earl of Elgin. While the Greeks continually call for their return, until and unless they are returned to Greece, they can be seen on display in the British Museum in London.

The Elgin Marbles in the British Museum, London © Flik47 / Shutterstock.com

1817 Death of Jane Austen

She lived from 1775-1817.

She was one of the greatest English novelists. Her most famous book is *Pride and Prejudice*.

She declared her strong sympathies for the Catholic Faith (and quite possibly died a Catholic).

The house in Winchester where Jane Austen lived and died.

1819 Peterloo Massacre

In 1819, a peaceful meeting in Manchester (St Peter's Fields) was broken up by soldiers wielding swords (this was before the days of police). Eleven were killed and 600 wounded. It became known as the Peterloo Massacre after St Peter's fields and the Battle of Waterloo four years earlier. The meeting was to call for the reform of Parliament.

1820 King George IV

He reigned as King from 1820-1830, but he had already been Prince Regent since 1811, when his father George III became incapable of ruling.

He is known as the Prince of Pleasure. One of his great, fashionable and flamboyant friends was Beau Brummell. He ran up enormous debts and was very fat and very unpopular.

His first and only true marriage was to Mrs Fitzherbert, a Catholic, but the state did not recognise it and insisted he marry his Protestant cousin Caroline of Brunswick, whom he never liked – he did not even invite her to his coronation.

He built the Royal Pavilion at Brighton and the term Regency is given to the furniture and buildings of this period.

The Royal Pavilion in Brighton © Don Simon © Shutterstock.com

Cato Street Conspiracy

This was a conspiracy, led by Thistlewood, to blow up the Cabinet in 1820. It failed and the leaders were arrested in Cato Street. The conspirators were against government policy which included parliamentary reform and Catholic emancipation.

Rosetta Stone decoded

This slab of black basalt, found by Napoleon's army in 1799 in Egypt, was surrendered to the British and presented to the British Museum in 1802. It contains hieroglyphs in both Egyptian and Greek which enabled archaeologists to translate many other hieroglyphic writings.

The Rosetta Stone © Vladimir Korostyshevskiy © Shutterstock.com

1820s Raffles

Sir Thomas Stamford Raffles established a trading port in Singapore. He founded the Zoological Society of London (London Zoo).

1824 National Gallery in London founded

This institution moved to its present building in Trafalgar Square in 1838, seen here behind Nelson's Column.

Trafalgar Square, London

1825 First Steam Train

George Stephenson built his steam engine, the Rocket, which pulled carriages the 15 miles between Stockton and Darlington in Northern England. Richard Trevithick built the first ever steam locomotive for industrial use in 1804, but Stephenson's design set the standard for the steam locomotives that followed.

A replica of Stevenson's Rocket © Meoita / Shutterstock.com

1826 First photograph

The first elementary photograph was taken by Joseph Niepse in France. However it was not until 1851 that the foundations of modern photography were properly established by Daguerre (Daguerreotypes) and William Fox Talbot who successfully exposed a negative in 1835.

An example of a daguerreotype thanks to Jan Weijers ©

1829 Catholic Emancipation Act

The British government reluctantly began to grant concessions to British and Irish Catholics who were thereafter able to become Members of Parliament and achieve high office in Ireland. William Pitt the Younger had tried to bring this measure about nearly thirty years before, but failed, and resigned from office shortly afterwards. Within a few years (1833), the Oxford Movement began, under John Keble, John Henry Newman and Edward Bouverie Pusey. This movement began to emphasise the Catholic principles on which they claimed the Church of England rested. However, in 1845, Newman converted to the Catholic Church and in 1879 he was made Cardinal.

The Boat Race

The Oxford and Cambridge Boat Race was first rowed on the River Thames at Henley in 1829, but was moved to its present course in London in 1836.

First Horse-drawn Bus service

London started its first horse-drawn bus service between Paddington and Bank.

1830 King William IV

He was George IV's younger brother and reigned from 1830-1837.

The main event of his reign was the passing of the Great Reform Bill.

1832 The Great Reform Bill

Parliament was full of members who had been elected by very few votes. Very few people had the right to vote and some large towns had no representatives.

Some members represented "rotten boroughs" with no inhabitants at all, like Old Sarum. Old Sarum is the impressive remains of an Iron Age hill fort two miles north of Salisbury and the site of that town's first Cathedral.

But Parliament, having seen the disasters brought on France by the French Revolution, did not favour reform, thinking it too was revolution.

The first person to press seriously for this reform was John Wilkes MP in 1776.

The first Reform Bill was defeated in 1831.

Two other Reform Bills were also defeated in 1831, but eventually the Duke of Wellington persuaded the House of Lords to accept it and the bill was passed, the King signing it in 1832.

The chief provisions were:

(1) a much fairer distribution of seats
(2) many more people having the vote.

Death of Sir Walter Scott

Scott was a famous Romantic Scottish author – Ivanhoe being one of his best known stories, dealing with the Age of Chivalry. He is also famous for his Waverley Novels.

1833 Abolition of the Slave Trade

A slave is a person who is owned completely by another person. Slaves were bought and sold like any other property. The ancient Greeks and Romans had slaves, and in 73BC a gladiator called Spartacus led a rebellion of slaves. The Negro slave trade, which began in the 15th Century, involved shipping slaves from Africa (who had been sold by their chiefs) to Brazil, the West Indies and North America. They were used to cultivate the land and it has recently been revealed that the trade was often facilitated by merchant ships under the control of the bankers. Thanks in part to William Wilberforce, the Slave Trade was forbidden in 1807 by England, and in 1833 slavery was abolished in all British Colonies. In the USA, after the publication of Uncle Tom's Cabin, the Northern States decided against slavery. The Southern States were still in favour, and this division led to the American Civil War in 1865, which the Northern States won.

The Industrial Revolution

This began in the eighteenth century and marks the change from people working at home to working in factories.

The first invention of note was James Watts' improved steam engine in 1782. This was closely associated with -

Kay's Flying Shuttle – weaving faster

Hargreaves' Spinning Jenny – making yarn

Cartwright's Power Loom – wool and cotton.

All the inventions needed steel and heat from burning coal to shape the steel. Thus at the hub of the Industrial Revolution lay the iron and coal industries.

Manchester became the capital of the cotton industry and Birmingham of the metal trades. The countryside began to empty.

Houses were needed quickly and cheaply and were thus put up with little thought, giving rise to row upon row of dreary housing and numerous sanitation problems.

Better transport was soon needed and James Brindley was one of the first canal builders. By 1800, the enormous network of canals linking the important towns had begun to grow.

The Grand Western Canal at Sampford Peverell, Devon

John McAdam invented tarmac and Rennie and Telford built better bridges.

George Stephenson built a steam engine, the Rocket, that could move on rails, and in 1825 the first railway line opened between Stockton and Darlington. Within 20 years, all the main towns were connected by railway and the canals began to fall into disrepair.

Next came steam ships which replaced sailing ships. The first was the Comet on the River Clyde.

With machinery doing so much work, women and children worked long hours in the factories until the Factory Acts introduced more humane practices.

Factory workers formed themselves into Trade Unions, although it was not until 1871 that Trade Unions were allowed to help the workers legally.

The Industrial Revolution saw a population shift from the open south to the industrial north of England.

In short this was the century of the Industrial Revolution, whereby a simple slow-moving way of life was transformed into a materialistic and complicated one. Inventions included:

Other famous engineers and inventors who should be mentioned include:

- Richard Trevithick, whose work started the widespread use of steam engines
- Thomas Newcomen from Devon, who invented the first practical steam engine for pumping water
- Isambard Kingdom Brunel, probably the most famous Victorian engineer who built ships, the most famous of which being SS Great Britain, launched in 1843 and which can still be visited in Bristol

SS Great Britain in Bristol

- Brunel also planned railway tracks and built some striking bridges, many of which still survive, in use, today

Brunel's iconic railway bridge spanning the River Tamar at Saltash, Cornwall.

- Abraham Darby (died 1717), who invented a vastly improved method of producing pig iron (for rails in railways) using a blast furnace that burned coke instead of charcoal. His grandson, with the same name, was the architect of the first Iron Bridge at Coalbrookdale in Shropshire, opened 1781

Iron Bridge at Ironbridge, Shropshire © Steve Cordory / Shutterstock.com

- Henry Bessemer, who developed a process for the mass production of steel in 1865
- Celsius, who developed a temperature scale in Sweden in the eighteenth century
- Alessandro Volta, Italy, who developed the battery as a reliable source of electric energy

Arguably the most important development of the Industrial Revolution was the creation of a network of railways because it was these that enabled the goods produced by the factories to be transported and distributed far more widely than was possible during the days of the horse and cart. Railways also enabled people to visit places they had only been able to walk to, or ride to, before.

The Factories Act

Working conditions were so bad that, with the inspiration and efforts of the Earl of Shaftesbury, the Factories Act of 1833 was passed to protect workers of all ages. For example, it ruled that:

- no children under the age of nine could work in factories
- children under 13 should work for no more than 8 hours a day
- women and those under 18 should work for no more than 12 hours a day

Tolpuddle Martyrs
Six farm workers from Tolpuddle in Dorset, England, were transported to Tasmania for administering illegal oaths and for forming a trade union. Their sentence was eventually remitted, but, in time, this event led to the development of the Chartist Movement in 1838, which called for political reform and ultimately led indirectly to the formation of the British Labour Party in 1900.

Tamworth Manifesto
Sir Robert Peel, in a speech to a gathering of the Tory party in the town of Tamworth in 1834, issued his manifesto in which he set forth his vision of a new liberal conservatism, resulting in the Tory party changing its name to the Conservative party.

Statue of Sir Robert Peel in Bury, Lancashire, where he was the Member of Parliament. Thanks to Alex Blatchford ©.

Palace of Westminster burned down
This building, also known as the Houses of Parliament, was rebuilt in its present Gothic Revival design under the architectural supervision of Charles Barry and Augustus Pugin.

The Palace of Westminster, London

1835 First Computer
The first computer was conceived by Charles Babbage, who lived in Totnes, Devon. His "analytical engine" was finally built in 1991.

Death of John Nash
This famous British architect, who was born in 1752, created many famous buildings, including Buckingham Palace and The Royal Pavilion in Brighton also designed the layout of Regent Street in London.

Regent Street, London

The Great Trek

The Boer (Dutch) settlers in South Africa began to move to the North and East of the River Orange to escape British rule.

1836 John Constable dies

This English landscape painter from Suffolk had been born in 1776.

Chartists

After the passing of the Great Reform Bill in 1832, the London Working Men's Association was formed, which drew up a charter calling for: (a) every man to have a vote; (b) equal-sized constituencies; (c) anyone to be eligible to stand for Parliament; (d) MPs to be paid; (e) annual elections.

Parliament refused to agree and the more extreme Chartists in 1836 led an armed revolt. Many Chartists died in this unsuccessful revolt and, as a result, a monster petition of 2 million signatures was prepared. This was seized and many names discovered to be forgeries. In spite of their failure, within 70 years the first four demands became law.

1837 Queen Victoria

She reigned from 1837-1901. She married Albert of Saxe-Coburg who died in 1861.

The Albert Memorial, London

Famous events during Queen Victoria's reign:

- The Chartists
- Great Exhibition
- Crimean War
- Indian Mutiny
- Income Tax was introduced permanently
- American Civil War
- Franco-Prussian War
- General Gordon in the Sudan
- Highland Clearances
- County & Parish Councils
- Boer War
- Her own Diamond Jubilee

Famous people during her reign:

- Sir Robert Peel
- Lord Palmerston
- Gladstone
- Disraeli

1838 First Afghan War

There were three Afghan Wars (1838-42, 1878-80 and 1919), fought by Britain against Russia, partly to prevent Russia advancing into India and partly to try to subdue the rebellious Ghilzai.

Grand National

This race was first run at Aintree, Liverpool. The most famous Grand National Horse was Red Rum which won in 1973, 1974 and 1977, coming second in 1975 and 1976.

Grace Darling

This lady, aged 23, and daughter of a lighthouse keeper, is famed for rescuing five people from their wrecked ship on the Farne Islands off the coast of Northumberland in her rowing boat.

1839 Henley Royal Regatta

This was held for the first time this year. It is arguably the most beautiful annual sporting event that is held in Britain

Henley Royal Regatta from the air.
With kind permission of the Stewards of the Henley Royal Regatta©

Opium Wars

The first of these lasted from 1839 to 1842. It was between Britain and China and it started when the Chinese government confiscated the British Opium stores in Canton in an attempt to end the British monopoly of the trade in this drug in parts of China. This event was followed by British sailors murdering a Chinese official. The Chinese army was severely weakened by opium addiction and the British soon won the war. The ending was formalised by the Treaty of Nanking, in which the British were granted rights to expand the opium monopoly to several designated offshore islands.

When the British demanded the right to sell opium throughout mainland China, the Chinese resisted, whereupon the British attacked, thus starting the second Opium War, which lasted from 1856 until 1860. It was fought between Britain and France on the one side and China on the other. The consequence of these wars was that the British were indeed granted the right to the monopoly in the mainland and thus opium was legalised throughout China.

David Sassoon was the man who administered the British monopoly. Ships that had taken opium from Afghanistan to China would return to Britain laden with tea.

Bicycle invented

Kirkpatrick Macmillan, from Dumfries in Scotland, invented the modern bicycle with pedals and brakes.

1840 Entente Cordiale

During the nineteenth century, colonial expansion by both France and Britain caused tension between the two nations. To counteract this, diplomats established the "Entente Cordiale," an expression that can be traced back to this date. It was an informal term used to describe the close relationship and co-operation that then began to develop between Britain and France.

Irish Potato Famine

Catholic Ireland longed for independence from Protestant Britain, and this longing was increased by the terrible suffering of the Potato Famine in the 1840s. Almost 1 million people died and a further million emigrated.

First Postage Stamp

In 1840, postage stamps were introduced. Rowland Hill, afterwards Sir Rowland, persuaded the government to reduce the postage to 1d on letters between all places in the United Kingdom. Rowland Hill's suggestion was not only accepted, but followed by every other civilized country in the World.

A Penny Black Stamp © Doctor Jools / Shutterstock.com

1842 Penal Settlements in Australia

These were set up after 1842 for British convicts sentenced to transportation to Australia. Life in them was particularly harsh.

Income Tax Introduced permanently

While income tax had been first introduced in 1799 to finance the Napoleonic wars, in 1842 Sir Robert Peel introduced income tax of 7d in the pound on all who earned more than £150 a year. It was meant to last three years, but in 1845 it was renewed and the British public have been paying it ever since.

1843 Telegraph

The first Telegraph service began between Paddington and Slough. This was followed by the US invention in the following year (1844) of the Morse Code, by Samuel Morse.

1846 Repeal of the Corn Laws

The repeal of the Corn Laws ushered in world-wide free trade, the effect of which was to impoverish Britain and Ireland through cheap imports. The only part of the British Isles to benefit from this was the City of London, which became the financial capital of the world.

Two further developments of this world trade:
1) The British Empire became arguably the greatest empire the world has ever seen.
2) The financial institutions in the City of London needed to know what was going on around the world, so they could influence events, and this led to them starting their own intelligence service which, in due course, would become the nation's secret services in 1909.

Sir Robert Peel

He was Prime Minister once during Queen Victoria's reign. He eventually supported Catholic emancipation. He is credited with being the originator of the Conservative Party. He founded the Metropolitan Police Force in London, in 1829, and is the reason policemen are still called Bobbies.

1848 Marx & Engels

Marx and Engels, who both worked in England, published their famous book, *The Communist Manifesto*, in 1848 – the last words of this book being: "Workers of the world unite." Their main tenet was that the value of an article or service is based on the time taken to supply it, which was directly contrary to the theory of Value Pricing. Employed by a secret society (translated as the "League of Just men"), Marx and Engels devised policies that went beyond Socialism, a movement that was considered, by many at that time, to be a more-or-less respectable concept; they called for the overthrow of both society's representative government, as well as the Church, through plunder, violence and deceit; in time these policies were to lead to the mass murder of millions of workers in Russia (Soviet Union), but did nothing to improve their lot. In 1867, Marx wrote *Das Kapital*.

1850 The Height of the Pre-Raphaelite Painting Brotherhood

These British painters wanted to shun the influence of all artists after Raphael and to try to emulate Italian painters before him. Their most famous members were Rosetti, Millais, Holman Hunt and William Morris. Closely associated with them was the art critic John Ruskin. In part they had drawn their inspiration from the Nazarenes, a group of Dutch and German painters who worked in Italy at the beginning of the 19th century.

William Wordsworth

This English poet started life with strong republican beliefs, but later developed both a conservative outlook as well as feelings of mystical union with the countryside. He died on St George's Day, 1850. He was born in 1770.

1851 Great Exhibition

This was held in 1851 at the suggestion of Prince Albert. It was the first ever great trade exhibition. Manufacturers from all over the world brought and exhibited their goods. It was held in a huge glass palace (Crystal Palace) which was built in Hyde Park, but later removed to Crystal Palace in South London.

Turner dies

Joseph William Mallord Turner, the great English landscape painter was born in 1775.

1853 Crimean War

In 1853, Tsar Nicholas I of Russia claimed he should protect all Christians in the land ruled by Turkey, but Turkey ignored his claim. The Tsar sent troops to protect the Christians and Turkey declared war, but the Russians destroyed the Turkish fleet in the Black Sea. Britain and France, fearing Russia would become too powerful, sent troops to attack the Crimea.

The British won the Battle of Alma in 1854, but failed to take the main city of Sebastopol. The Russians then besieged Balaclava. During the siege, the Charge of the Light Brigade took place at which British Cavalry attacked the wrong guns and suffered appalling casualties. The last main battle saw another British victory at Inkerman.

The war ended in stalemate because atrocious weather and inefficient provisioning caused heavy British casualties, although it is usually reported as a British and French victory.

The war is famous for the nursing work of Florence Nightingale, but credit should also be given to Sister Bridgeman and the Catholic Sisters of Mercy.

1856 Victoria Cross

This award, the highest award for military heroism, was instituted this year. The medals are struck from canons used in the Crimea War (See also 1915.)

© Image provided with kind permission of Iain Stewart of Victoria Cross.org

1857 Indian Mutiny

In 1857, Indian Sepoys (Indians serving in the British Army) tried to throw out the East India Company and regain independence for India.
One aspect of Indian resentment against the British was the use by the British of cow fat in rifle bullets – the cow in India is a sacred animal to the Hindus.
The mutiny broke out in Delhi which was captured by the Indians. The British, Europeans and Sikhs then laid siege to the town which they recaptured after four months. There were other sieges at Cawnpore and Lucknow. The British recaptured both, but with dreadful loss of life to the civilians inside.
The fighting finished in 1858, but from then on India was ruled by the British Government and not the East India Company. British rule, which would last until 1947, is commonly referred to as the British Raj, or Indian Empire, with Queen Victoria becoming Empress of India.

1859 The Origin of Species

This work, *On the Origin of Species by Means of Natural Selection*, written by Charles Darwin, was published and launched the theory of Evolution. Its publication aroused bitter controversy because the view that species evolve as a result of mutations was seen to conflict with both biblical creation as well as the conclusions of the Austrian friar and founder of the science of genetics, Gregor Mendel. Alfred Russell, a contemporary of Darwin's, said that Mendel's discoveries, which were supported by laboriously collected scientific evidence, were a serious threat to Darwin's theory because Darwin's views were merely a series of assumptions that had not been proved by observation.

Big Ben

This famous bell, which was recast from its short-lived predecessor (which cracked within two years of being cast), was hung in its present home, St Stephen's Tower, at the north end of the Houses of Parliament.

Lord Palmerston

He was a famous Prime Minister from 1859 to 1865.
He was a Whig who was also famous as a foreign minister, particularly colonising Hong Kong for Great Britain, taking control of it from the Chinese.

1860 The Open (the first British Open Golf Championship)
The first Open Golf Championship was held at Prestwick in Scotland. The game of golf originated in Britain.

1868 Benjamin Disraeli
He was probably the most famous Victorian prime minister. He was prime minister twice (in 1868 and between 1874 and 1880). He wrote novels – particularly Coningsby. He was a Jew who became a Christian. His main rival was William Gladstone. He bought all the shares in the Suez Canal in 1875. He died in 1881.

William Gladstone
He was four times Prime Minister during Queen Victoria's reign (see appendices for the dates) – but the Queen did not like him.
He was originally a Conservative under Sir Robert Peel, but, due to his liberal ideas, particularly trying to abolish Income Tax, he broke away from the Conservatives to form the Liberal Party in 1868. His main failure was his inability to get the Home Rule for Ireland Bill passed in the House of Commons. Had he succeeded, the problems of Northern Ireland in the 20th Century might not have arisen. He died in 1898.

1869 Cutty Sark
The most famous ship used in transporting tea from the east to Britain is a tea clipper, the Cutty Sark. It was built in 1869 and can still be visited in Greenwich. She was one of last such ships to be built and also one of the fastest

The hull of the Curry Sark as it appears today © John Braid / Shutterstock.com

1870 Charles Dickens

He lived from 1812-1870.

He is one of the greatest English novelists. His books include: The Pickwick Papers, David Copperfield, Oliver Twist, Great Expectations, A Tale of Two Cities, Barnaby Rudge (set during the Gordon Riots).

FA Cup first held and RFU formed

It was in this year that the Rugby Football Union was formed. In 1890, Rugby school claimed that this game had been invented there when, in 1823, William Webb Ellis picked up the ball in a game of what is now called football (or soccer).

In 1883, England, Scotland, Wales and Ireland began the "Home Nations" Rugby Championships. France joined in 1910 ("Five Nations") and Italy in 1997 ("Six Nations").

In 1895, the world of Rugby was split when the Northern clubs formed what became known in 1922 as the Rugby League. In 1906, the League game reduced the numbers of players from 15 to 13.

1873 Death of John Stuart Mill

Mill was a British philosopher, political theorist and sometime MP, who advocated Utilitarianism and women's suffrage. His most famous work was *On Liberty*.

1876 Telephone

The telephone, which had been invented by Scottish-born US scientist Alexander Graham Bell in 1872, was granted its first patent in 1876. Bell also invented the gramophone in 1887.

1877 Wimbledon and Test Cricket

The first men's singles tennis championship was held this year. It was also the year of the first cricket test match between England and Australia in Melbourne.

1879 Zulu War

This South African war ended in defeat for the Zulus by the British, with Zululand being incorporated into the Natal. With the Zulus defeated, the Boers were then encouraged to throw off British occupation of the Transvaal (a province in Northern South Africa which the British had annexed in 1877). This resistance led to the Boer War, 1899-1902 (see later). There were three important battles in the Zulu War:

- The siege of Rorke's Drift, when 140 British soldiers held off more than 4,000 Zulu warriors

Rorke's Drift ©Joseph Sohm / Shuterstock.com

- Isandhlwana, a few miles from Rorke's Drift and fought earlier on the same day – a Zulu victory
- Ulundi, which gave the British victory

1881 Savoy Theatre and Gilbert & Sullivan

The theatre was built by Richard D'Oyly Carte to present the comic operas of W. S. Gilbert (librettist) and Arthur Sullivan (composer). There are fourteen Gilbert and Sullivan operas and they were written between 1871 and 1896. This was the first public building in England to be lit by electricity, with electric street lighting following shortly afterwards.

1884 General Charles Gordon

He is famous for his exploits in China and the Sudan. He is mainly remembered for organising the Sudan, being made Governor General in 1877. He wiped out the slave trade there. He was a devoted Evangelical, who visited the sick and set

up a boys' club in Kent, though apparently some of his beliefs were rather eccentric (including in reincarnation).
In 1884, while trying to lead the defeated Egyptian army out of the Sudan, he was besieged in Khartoum. He was killed two days before British troops came to relieve him.

Madame Tussauds
This waxwork museum opened in its present site in Marylebone Rd in London. The neighbouring Planetarium opened in 1958, but has since closed.

Brompton Oratory
This massive Baroque Catholic church, inspired by Father Faber, was the largest place of Catholic worship in London, until Westminster Cathedral was completed in 1903.

The Brompton Oratory in London

Greenwich Meridian
This was accepted as the Prime Meridian or 0 degrees longitude from which the standard times of different areas of the world were calculated. In 1986, this was succeeded by Co-ordinated Universal Time.

1886 Joe Chamberlain
He was a prominent liberal who broke away to start his own party, the Unionist Association, because he favoured Ireland being united to Britain. This association then merged with the Conservative party. Chamberlain was against

Home Rule for Ireland. He had two sons, Austen and Neville, the latter being famous for signing the Munich agreement.

1888 James Keir Hardie

He formed the Scottish Labour Party, which eventually developed into the (British) Labour Party in 1920.

Local Councils.

County Councils were set up to run the counties in 1888. Parish Councils were set up in 1894.

1890 Forth Railway Bridge completed

Forth Rail Bridge © David Head / Shutterstock.com

1891 Baccarat Scandal

The Prince of Wales, the future Edward VII, had been present at a game of Baccarat at Tranby Croft, near Hull, at which one of the players had been accused of cheating. The Prince appeared as a witness in the ensuing libel case.

Death of Joseph Bazalgette

This Englishman rebuilt the London sewers, which resulted in greatly improved air quality in the city. The surface buildings associated with his work still stand and have a character all of their own. He also was responsible for the building of the London Embankment.

A building associated with Sir Joseph Bazalgette © Kiev Victor / Shutterstock.com

1894 Tower Bridge (in London) opened

Tower Bridge, London

1895 Promenade Concerts (The Proms)

Sir Henry Wood organised the first of these now world-famous annual concert seasons in the Royal Albert Hall, London.

Royal Albert Hall in London

Jameson Raid

During the nineteenth century, British settlers dominated South Africa running it as a Cape Colony. The Dutch, called Boers, resented this and crossed the Vaal River to form their own Transvaal Republic, or South African Republic, in 1840. The British Government in 1880 annexed Transvaal which led to fighting in which the Boers were victorious.

Shortly after gold and diamonds were discovered in the Transvaal and, in order to protect this find, the Boers refused to allow non-Boers any rights.

In 1895 Dr Jameson led an armed force to protect the so-called outlanders in Transvaal, but President Kruger forced him to surrender at Krugersdorp.

The raid led to bad feeling between the British and the Boers and culminated in the Boer War (1899-1902).

1898 Battle of Omdurman

Anglo-Egyptian forces under General Horatio Kitchener, with modern weapons, effectively defeated the forces of Caliph Abd Allah. He was the Sudanese leader and the successor of the Mahdi and his army was known as the Caliphate. Kitchener conquered the Sudan and recaptured Khartoum.

1899 The Boer War

This war lasted from 1899-1902.

It resulted from the ill-feeling caused by the Jameson raid, but in essence it was caused by the rivalry over gold and diamond mines at Kimberley.

Until 1900, the Boers were winning the war under leaders such as Jan Smuts. When Lord Kitchener arrived, the British began to win. They recaptured Kimberley and relieved the towns of Mafeking and Ladysmith. President Kruger left South Africa and, while the war then ended, the Boers continued fighting as guerrillas until 1902, when they finally surrendered.

The British did not treat the Boers at all well, especially in the concentration camps they devised for the women and children, where many thousands died. In reparation, Britain gave £3million to help rebuild the country.

1901 Radio broadcasting invented

In 1901, Marconi transmitted the first transatlantic radio signal from the Lizard Peninsular in Cornwall to the USA. This peninsular was used again in 1962 when the Post Office built its radio dishes at nearby Goonhilly Down for receiving signals from space satellites.

The Radio dishes at Goonhilly, Cornwall © Stephen Gibson / Shutterstock.com

British Labour Party

This political party, whose roots go back to the Tolpuddle Martyrs, was formed as the Labour Representation Committee this year. It changed its name to the Labour Party in 1906.

Death of Queen Victoria

Queen Victoria was born in 1819 and ascended the throne in 1837. Her sense of duty and strict moral code came to symbolise the ethos of the 19th century. She married her cousin, Prince Albert of Saxe-Coburg-Gotha, who died in 1861. Her close friendship with the conservative Prime Minister, Benjamin Disraeli, who created her Empress of India in 1876, contrasted with the tension that existed between her and Disraeli's Liberal rival, William Gladstone. She is buried at Frogmore Mausoleum.

Commonwealth of Australia

In this year, the six colonies of Australia, (New South Wales, Victoria, Queensland, South Australia, Western Australia and Tasmania) were federated to form the Commonwealth of Australia, thus becoming an independent dominion of the British Empire.

Step 9. The House of Windsor (1901 to the Present Day)

(This royal house was called Saxe-Coburg Gotha until 1917 when its name was changed to Windsor.)

1901 King Edward VII

He reigned from 1901-1910.
His reputation was that of a fun-loving, but naughty King.
During his reign, Kaiser Wilhelm (Kaiser Bill), his own nephew, whom he thoroughly disliked, built up German arms in preparation for World War I.

King Edward VII © Everett Historical / Shutterstock.com

The architecture of this period is known as Edwardian and one of the best examples of this can be found at Stafford Terrace in London.

Stafford Terrace in London

1909 North Pole reached

US Polar explorer Robert Peary was the first to reach the North Pole. He beat the Norwegian Roald Amundsen who, in 1903/06 was the first to discover the North West Passage. In 1910, Amundsen was the first to reach the South Pole, a few days ahead of British Captain Scott.

1910 King George V

He reigned from 1910 -1936.
He married Princess Mary of Teck who died in 1953.
The main events of his reign were:

- World War I
- Suffragettes
- Balfour Declaration
- General Strike
- The loss of the Titanic
- It was he who began the Royal Christmas broadcasts

King George V inspecting troops © Everett Historical / Shutterstock.com

Kipling's poem *If*

This was also the year in which Rudyard Kipling wrote this famous poem.

1911 Siege of Sidney Street

This was a gunfight in Sidney Street, London, that resulted in the deaths of two politically motivated burglars. It is famous for the controversial involvement, at the scene, of Home Secretary, Winston Churchill, as well as the deaths of three policemen and a firefighter

1912 Titanic sank

RMS Titanic, which was reputed to be an unsinkable ship, did exactly that on her maiden voyage with the loss of over 1,500 lives.

A lifeboat carrying survivors from the Titanic © Everett Historical / Shutterstock.com

Sliced Bread

This was the year in which a machine for slicing bread was invented, which might be of interest, bearing in mind the often used expression, "[X] is the best thing since sliced bread."

Harrods Department Store opened

Harrods Department Store in London

1913 Crossword puzzle

This was the year that saw the first publication of a crossword puzzle, by Englishman Arthur Wynne, in US newspaper, *The New York World.* Britain was to follow in 1924.

1914 World War I

It lasted from 1914-1918.

It began when Archduke Franz Ferdinand the heir to the Austrian throne was murdered by a Serb at Sarajevo, in Serbia, which Austria had seized.

- The Austrians replied by attacking the Serbs
- So Russia came to the defence of Serbia
- Germany therefore attacked Russia
- France then came to Russia's aid
- Germany therefore defended itself by entering Belgium to attack France
- Britain decided to defend Belgium

It was an example of the Domino effect.

The war was fought in three main areas: the Western Front (West of Germany), The Eastern Front (East of Germany) and the Middle East, notably in Palestine where the strategy was to defeat the Turks and thus begin to make way for the creation of the State of Israel.

The Eastern Front

The Eastern Front saw fighting between Russia and Germany, but not with trench warfare.

When Turkey joined the German forces, Churchill decided to send British, Australian and New Zealand troops (The ANZACs) to knock Turkey out of the war and try to secure access to the Mediterranean for Russia.

The Gallipoli Landings

The allied forces landed at Gallipoli on 25th April 1915, but failed to make any real headway and were withdrawn in January 1916. This area is called the Underbelly of Europe.

The landing of the Lancashire Fusiliers at Gallipoli by Charles Dixon with kind permission of the trustees of the Fusilier Museum in Bury©

It was during the initial landing on the beach portrayed here (W Beach) that, possibly, the most famous awarding of Victoria Crosses (VCs) took place when the Lancashire Fusiliers won "6 VCs before breakfast." W Beach is now known as the Lancashire Landing.

As already intimated, one of the main purposes of World War I was to push the Turks out of Palestine. With the help of Lawrence of Arabia, who enlisted Arab support, General Allenby took Jerusalem in 1917 and from then until 1948 Palestine was under British control.

On the Western Front:
The German advance on France was halted by their defeat at the Battle of the Marne. Both sides dug trenches and stayed more or less stationary until the end of the War.

The British tried to break the deadlock in 1916 by attacking the German trenches in the Battle of the Somme. Field Marshall Haig was in charge but, using too few tanks, the allies lost 615,000 casualties and the Germans 650,000.

The memorial at Thiepval near the River Somme in France © Iconix / Shutterstock.com

When the Germans attacked Verdun in 1916, the French counter-attacked and eventually regained most of their lost ground.

In 1917, Haig's forces attacked Ypres, but this battle, like the Somme, only ended in huge casualties, mainly at Paschendale.

A view of part of the Tyne Cot Cemetery which lies below Paschendale, near Ypres. With kind permission of the Common-wealth War Graves Commission ©

In 1917, the Russian Revolution caused a complete allied collapse on the Eastern Front. This released Germans to fight on the Western Front and allowed them to attack US shipping with their submarines and U-Boats. This caused The United States of America to join the war and the extra troops soon gave the allies the upper hand.
Around the world the British Navy was attacking German colonies and this explains why there was fighting off the coast of South America, at the battles of Coronel and the Falkland Islands.
The two main fleets met at the Battle of Jutland in 1916. The fact that the German High Fleet never put to sea again afterwards emphasises the importance of this British victory.
World War I saw the start of air warfare. The Germans used airships called Zeppelins to start with, but both sides eventually used fighters, bombers, reconnaissance planes and even aircraft carriers.
Eventually the Germans were starved of food and lost heart over the war. Their leaders signed the Armistice (surrender) on 11th November 1918.
Germany lost all its colonies at the Treaty of Versailles. The Austrian Empire was shredded by the creation or enlargement of Czechoslovakia, Poland, Romania, Yugoslavia, Estonia, Latvia and Lithuania.
At the end of the war, all the countries, except the United States, formed the League of Nations to keep world peace. This, together with the Treaty of Versailles, was organised by US President Woodrow Wilson, British Prime Minister David Lloyd George and the French President Georges Clemenceau.
Finally, the German fleet was taken by the British to Scapa Flow in the Orkneys and sunk.
By the time the Armistice was signed on 11th November, 8 ½ million men had been killed, of which 888,246 are believed to have been either British or British Commonwealth (as it later became); and 21 million wounded.

1915 Shackleton's Boat Journey

In 1915, Sir Ernest Shackleton's ship, *Endurance*, was crushed in the South Polar ice. To save his crew, after they had drifted with the ice for some months, Shackleton led them in lifeboats over hundreds of miles of stormy seas to the nearest land and eventual safety. The perilous journey lasted many months, but every man was saved. The exciting story is one of the most impressive feats of leadership and risk-taking in modern history. The James Caird, the lifeboat in which the most perilous part of journey was undertaken, can still be seen at Shackleton's old school, Dulwich College in London.

The James Caird on display at Dulwich College.
With kind permission of the Governors of Dulwich College ©

1916 Ireland

In 1916, during Easter week, the Irish Republican Brotherhood claimed independence from Britain, but this rising was ruthlessly put down by the British. The famous Irish nationalist Sir Roger Casement was hanged for his part in the rising.

In 1920, and on the advice of Winston Churchill, the British used a new, temporary but brutal police force known as the Black and Tans.

British Summer Time introduced

Lloyd George

Liberal David Lloyd George, a Welshman, succeeded Herbert Asquith as Prime Minister in 1916. Earlier, as Chancellor of the Exchequer, he introduced Old Age Pensions and National Insurance. He was also Minister for War before becoming Prime Minister. He attended the Treaty of Versailles and resigned as Prime Minister in 1922.

The statue erected in memory of Lloyd George in Parliament Square © Anshar / Shutterstock.com

1917 Balfour Declaration

In a short letter from the British Foreign Secretary to Lord Rothschild, A. J. Balfour declared British support for the Zionists' call for a home for the Jews in the State of Palestine. However it has since been claimed that Balfour's wording was never meant to imply that the Palestinians should be evicted from their country, nonetheless this has indeed come to pass, and with disastrous consequences. (Zionism is the political movement founded in the late 19th century, the aim of which was to establish a homeland for Diaspora Jews to return to Palestine, and thus to create a Jewish State. At the Versailles Peace Conference in 1920, Britain was granted the mandate to bring this controversial creation about.)

During the period of the British Mandate in Israel, Irgun and its breakaway movement, the Stern gang, both of them guerrilla groups, carried out a number of anti-British atrocities, notably Irgun's attack on the King David Hotel in Jerusalem in 1946.

Commonwealth War Graves Commission

This year also saw the establishment of what is now known as the Commonwealth War Graves Commission, an organisation that tends nearly one million war graves and memorials around the world.

Another view of the Tyne Cot Cemetery, run by the Commonwealth War Graves Commission.
© Paul Daniels / Shutterstock.com

1918 Suffragettes

These were the campaigners, mainly women, for votes for women (women's suffrage). They were active, sometimes violently, between 1900 and 1918, when most women were given the vote. Their most famous leader was Emmeline Pankhurst and the most famous demonstration in favour of female suffrage was when Emily Davison killed herself by throwing herself in front of the horses in the 1913 Derby.

1919 Versailles

Even though Germany hadn't really lost the war, Britain and France wanted to ensure that Germany was thoroughly punished at the Versailles Peace Conference in 1919. Indeed, Lloyd George and the French leader Clemenceau wanted to prevent Germany from ever being a force in Europe again. In addition, President Woodrow Wilson of the USA would not negotiate with any unelected leader such as Charles of Austria. As a result of this somewhat intransigent attitude, the seeds of the Second World War were laid in this conference.

Part of The Palace of Versailles © Hung Chung Chih / Shutterstock.com

Nancy Astor

She was the first woman MP to be elected and take her seat in the British Parliament (In 1918, Constance Markievicz had been elected for the constituency of Dublin St Patrick's, but as a candidate for Sinn Fein she did not take up her seat in Parliament).

Amritsar Massacre

British troops in India killed 379 demonstrating, but unarmed, Sikhs without warning.

The Golden Temple at Amritsar © Aleksei Sarkisov / Shutterstock.com

Alcock and Brown

These two British aviators, Sir John Alcock and Sir Arthur Brown, made the first non-stop transatlantic flight in a Vickers-Vimy aircraft. The first proper plane to fly was built and flown by the Wright Brothers in 1903.

1920 Cenotaph

This memorial, designed by Sir Edwin Lutyens, was erected in Whitehall in London.

The Cenotaph in London © Valdis Skudre / Shutterstock.com

Chatham House founded

The more formal name of this organisation is the Royal Institute of International Affairs, and its purpose is to create a prosperous and secure world. When "Chatham House Rules" operate that means that, after a meeting has taken place, an attendee may reveal what has been said but may mention neither who said it nor who else was in attendance.

Home Rule Act

This act incorporated Northern Ireland (Ulster) into the United Kingdom. The rest of Ireland (the Irish Republic) became a dominion. This country became the Irish Free State or Eire in 1937

1921 Irish Free State

In 1921, the Irish Parliament, after the efforts of Michael Collins and Arthur Griffith, reluctantly agreed to the partitioning of Ireland. This involved the setting up of the Irish Free State, separated from the Northern six counties. The latter comprised Ulster which remained part of the United Kingdom of Great Britain and Northern Ireland, the somewhat lumpy entity that had been set up the year before. Michael Collins briefly became head of state but was killed in

1922. Eamon De Valera was a very prominent nationalist who became Prime Minister of Ireland (1932-48, 51-54, 57-59) and then President (1959-73).

First Birth Control Clinic opened in London by Marie Stopes

Chequers

It was in this year that this house in Buckinghamshire was given to the nation as a weekend retreat for British Prime Ministers and for them to use for entertaining, especially foreign dignitaries. Hitherto there had been no need for such a retreat because Prime Ministers had tended to come from the landed gentry and so already had their own country retreat.

1923 BBC

The British Broadcasting Corporation began regular radio broadcasts.

Wembley

The FA cup final was first held at Wembley. This stadium was knocked down in the late 1990s and replaced with a new stadium on the same site that held its first match in 2007.

Stanley Baldwin

He became Prime Minister (Conservative) in 1923 and was in office, with two small interruptions, until 1937. He was Prime Minister during the General Strike. He was also Prime Minister when Edward VIII abdicated. The main interruption to his rule was caused by Ramsay Macdonald (Labour) who led a national government from 1931 – 1935.

1924 First Socialist Government in Britain

The demise of the Liberal Party happened as a result of two things:

- The Unionists (who opposed home rule for Ireland) had broken away from the Liberals to join the Conservative Party
- Lloyd George's refusal to impose a tax on land. This failure to impose the Land Values measure created such resentment amongst the working classes that they rejected Liberalism as being far too weak

This resulted in the Labour Party, led by Ramsey MacDonald, being elected to power, though as a minority government, and one that only lasted nine months. It failed to win the next general election, in 1924, partly because of …

… The Zinoviev Letter

Grigory Zinoviev, chairman of Comintern, had apparently written to British Communists urging them to copy what had happened in Russia and start a revolution in Britain, and this rumour frightened the British electorate into returning a Conservative government in 1924 with a very large majority. In 1999 the British Foreign Office declared this letter to be a fake and merely part of the Tory attempt to prevent the Labour Party, under Ramsay MacDonald, winning the 1924 General Election. Nonetheless, Zinoviev said later that, if he had been asked to sign such a letter, he would have done so.

Television

The British electrical engineer and inventor John Logie Baird gave the first demonstration of television.

1926 General Strike

This occurred in 1926, when the whole British work force went on strike for 10 days. Stanley Baldwin was Prime Minister and during its course, with no newspapers, the government published the British Gazette.

Menin Gate Memorial

This memorial, the largest memorial commemorating those who died in World War I, was built in Ypres over the road that led to nearby Paschendale. To this day, at 8pm every evening the traffic is halted and the "Last Post" sounded. It commemorates over 50,000 who were killed in that part of Belgium and for whom there is no known grave. Seventy four years later, by November 2001, the "Last Post" had been sounded 25,000 times, but, as may be noted to further emphasise the appalling loss of life that it commemorates, after seventy four years, by that time, it had been sounded only once for just half of those whose names are on the memorial.

The Menin Gate Memorial at Ypres.
With kind permission of the Commonwealth War Graves Commission ©.

1928 Thomas Hardy dies

He was a famous British novelist whose works feature Dorset and the West of England.

1929 Penicillin first used in an operation

The use of penicillin was developed by Scottish bacteriologist Alexander Fleming. He is generally credited with the discovery of penicillin although there are a number of others who did a great deal more to promote its life-saving use than he did.

1931 British Commonwealth established

This is a loose association of 54 independent nations, most of which were formerly members of the British Empire. In 1947, it changed its name to the Commonwealth of Nations.

1933 Edward Elgar dies

This great English Catholic composer was born in 1857 and is associated with his home in the Malvern Hills, Worcestershire.

Glyndebourne presents its first opera

This opera house in Sussex was opened by John Christie.

The present day opera house at Glyndebourne.
© Glyndebourne Productions Ltd. Photo: Sam Stephenson

British Council

This organisation was established by the Government to represent British culture abroad, arranging visits and exhibitions by artists and performers.

1936 Edward VIII

He was the only monarch to give up the throne voluntarily. He succeeded his father, George V, in January 1936, but abdicated in December 1936 on his choice to marry Wallis Simpson, a divorcee. With the British Monarch being head of the Church of England, it was decided, he could not do this. He was a popular man, much given to the welfare of his subjects, and his abdication caused a great deal of unhappiness in the country. The man who most opposed the marriage was Stanley Baldwin.

King Edward VIII © EMKA74 / Shutterstock.com

King George VI

He reigned from 1936 to 1952, and therefore throughout the Second World War He did not expect to reign but did so when his elder brother Edward VIII abdicated. He was the last Emperor of India and the first Head of the Commonwealth. He married Lady Elizabeth Bowes-Lyon who, after his death, and until her death in 2002 was known as The Queen Mother. He was succeeded by his elder daughter Elizabeth II.

A postage Stamp depicting King George VI and Queen Elizabeth
© Sergey Goyachev / Shutterstock.com

1938 Munich Agreement

In 1938, the British Prime Minister, Neville Chamberlain, was assured by Hitler that the latter had no further ambitions in Europe; Chamberlain flew home with a sheet of paper to this effect signed by Hitler, with Chamberlain declaring "Peace in our time." This policy of giving way to the demands of a dictator and hoping that such agreements will bring peace is called "Appeasement." However, knowing of Hitler's intentions with regard to Poland, Chamberlain assured the Poles, and warned Hitler that if Germany invaded Poland, Britain would come to Poland's aid. No-one was quite sure why Britain gave this assurance. Some said that it was to please President Roosevelt, because it would secure him the Polish-American vote. If this were the case, Roosevelt cruelly betrayed this same country through his later subservience to Stalin.

Prime Minister Neville Chamberlain returning from Munich holding the piece of paper that Hitler had signed and which Chamberlain believed represented peace.(c)Everett Historical / Shutterstock.com

The Mallard

This was the year that the Mallard broke the world speed record for a steam train (125.88 miles per hour). This locomotive may be seen at the National Railway Museum in York.

The Mallard steam engine © Laurence Gough / Shutterstock.com

The fastest passenger service, between Cheltenham and London Paddington, was first set by the Cheltenham Flyer in 1929. This locomotive that pulled this train, Caerphilly Castle, may be seen at the Steam museum in Swindon.

Caerphilly Castle, the locomotive that pulled The Cheltenham Flyer

1939 to 1945 World War II

The Causes of the War:

Many Germans believed that they could have continued fighting after 1918. The German nation was humiliated at the Treaty of Versailles and had to give up much of its own territory.

The Germans thus deeply resented the way they had been treated, and particularly the economic hardship they suffered in the 1920s.

This was the seedbed into which Adolf Hitler was planted. He became Fuhrer in 1933 and was resolved not only to regain the lost German territory, but for Germany to become the greatest power on earth.

This explains why Germany invaded or occupied parts of Austria, Czechoslovakia and Poland, which had been German and in which many Germans were still living.

To begin with, Great Britain and France allowed Hitler to edge back into former territories, but in 1938, at Munich, Hitler agreed to move no further. Neville Chamberlain, British Prime Minister, thought Hitler would keep his word. When Hitler moved his troops into Poland, and especially because Great Britain had promised to defend Poland, were this to happen, Great Britain declared war on Germany in 1939.

It was obvious throughout the 1930s that Germany was preparing for war because of its massive rearmament.
Hitler was the head of the Nazi Party – the National Socialist German Workers Party.
Following Hitler's example of expansionism, Italy, under Mussolini, marched troops into Ethiopia and Japan invaded Manchuria. These countries formed the Axis powers.
The League of Nations was powerless to prevent the Axis powers' operations and was considered to be quite ineffective.

The Start of the War

The war really began on 3rd September 1939, when Germany invaded Poland.
Two weeks later, the USSR also invaded Poland, Estonia, Latvia and Lithuania.
The British troops that went to France were not faced with Germans and thus this period became known as "the Phoney War."
The first naval battle was the Battle of the River Plate, which ended when the German cruiser, Admiral Graf Spee left the port of Montevideo and was scuttled rather than engage the superior British and New Zealand force that awaited her.

The Graf Spee being scuttled © Everett Historical / Shutterstock.com

The French defences running north/south against Germany were called the Maginot Line.
In 1940, the Germans moved into Norway and Denmark, Belgium, Holland and Luxembourg.

The British troops on the Continent were trapped and had to escape from the beach at Dunkirk – 346,000 were picked up, partly by pleasure craft from England.

The evacuation of the British Expeditionary Force (B.E.F.) from Dunkirk in 1940. The troops are wading out to the rescuing vessel © REX/Shutterstock

Hitler then moved his troops into France which fell on 22nd June 1940.
In early summer 1940, Winston Churchill became Prime Minister.
Hitler then decided to invade England and began by bombing airfields and posts, but the British Spitfire and Hurricane RAF fighters were so successful in shooting down these bombers and sinking the barges collecting troops on the other side of the Channel that Germany was forced to give up its invasion plans. This air battle, fought between August and October 1940, is known as the Battle of Britain.
The Germans then restricted their attacks to bombing English cities and in London this was known as the Blitz. In 12 months, nearly 100,000 civilians were killed or wounded.

World War II – the North African Campaign
Much of North Africa was under Italian control and when, in June 1940, Italy joined Germany in the war, their fresh and complete army was able to begin enlarging their hold on North Africa.
In the autumn of 1940, the Italians invaded Egypt from Libya, but British forces under General Wavell pushed them back.
In 1941, the Germans fought south through Yugoslavia, Albania, Greece and Crete, leading to Germany landing in Libya to assist the Italians (the German leader was General Erwin Rommel).

The Germans advanced towards Egypt, taking Tobruk in 1941. Wavell was not to blame for this failure because his forces had been severely depleted by Churchill who had moved half of the British army into Greece. Nonetheless Wavell was replaced by Auchinleck, who was also successful, but made to take the blame for a later reversal of fortune. Auchinleck was replaced a few months later by General Montgomery (Monty) and, under the latter, the British 8th Army hit back in October by winning the crucial battle of El Alamein in 1942.

The Cross of Sacrifice at the Commonwealth War Graves Commission Cemetery at El Alamein. With many thanks to Ian Mcleod ©

From this point on the Germans were on the retreat, and in May 1943 they surrendered in North Africa.

From El Alamein the eighth army pushed the Germans west along the North African coast and then north through Sicily and up the Italian mainland. Italy surrendered in September 1943 and Rome was taken in June 1944. It was a turning point in the war.

World War II in General

Once Hitler had conquered central Europe, he resolved to crush the USSR.

He reached within 20 miles of Moscow in December 1941, but the cold, and the Russian armies, prevented him from progressing further and thus he never controlled the USSR.

By January 1943, the Russians were able to drive the Germans home and this was how the Russians re-entered Poland and Romania.

On 7th December 1941, the Japanese attacked Pearl Harbour in Hawaii, thus forcing the US into the War.

The Japanese attack on Pearl Harbour 7 December 1941 ©Rex/Shutterstock

Japan then took control of most of the western edge of the Pacific, including Hong Kong and Singapore.

After the Germans had lost the Graf Spee in 1939, and the Bismarck in 1941, their naval efforts centred around U-boat attacks on merchant ships taking food from North America to Britain and the USSR.

Meanwhile the RAF began heavy bombing raids on German industrial cities.

Between 1941 and 1945, escorted allied merchant ships delivered vital supplies to Archangel and Murmansk. They were known as the Arctic Convoys.

Once the Americans had joined the war, as had been the case at the end of World War I against Germany, their strength of numbers began to push the Japanese out of their conquered territories in the Pacific. The British pushed the Japanese out of Burma.

During the war British cryptologists were able to decipher a vast number of German messages on their Enigma machines at Bletchley Park.

Bletchley Park © Gordon Bell / Shutterstock.com

On 6th June 1944, a huge allied landing in Normandy (The Normandy landings, on D day), under General Eisenhower pushed the Germans back to Paris and eventually to Germany itself.

The remains of the temporary Mulberry Harbour constructed for the Normandy Landings that can still be seen off Arromanches today. With many thanks to Ben Mayne ©

Meanwhile the Germans had been sending pilotless flying bombs – V1s (like an aeroplane) or doodlebugs and V2s (rockets) – to London and these caused over 50,000 casualties.

The allies' advance up through Italy, coupled with both their push east across Northern Europe from Normandy as well as the Russians advancing west towards them, forced Germany to surrender in May 1945.

It is claimed Hitler committed suicide, and Churchill, Roosevelt and Stalin met at Yalta in the Crimea to organise the peace treaty.

Japan could only be made to surrender after the US had exploded atomic bombs over Hiroshima and Nagasaki in August 1945.

Russia took over most of Eastern Europe and East Germany, forcing a huge tract of land to become Communist – this lasted until 1990.

The German and Japanese leaders were tried for war crimes and many executed. Some notable German figures included Rommel (a highly decorated field marshal) , Admiral Dönitz (head of the German Navy), and Goering and Himmler (both leading members of the Nazi party).

About 384,000 British were killed in the war and in total over 35 million elsewhere.

1944 Education Act

This watershed Act in British education split secondary education into two levels, the Grammar Schools and the Secondary Modern Schools, both of which would be free for pupils. It raised the school leaving age to 15 (which was further increased to 16 in 1972). The result of a pupil taking the "Eleven Plus" exam at the age of 11, or over, would determine to which level of education he or she would progress after leaving Primary School. This Act is sometimes called the Butler Act after R. A. Butler, the president of the Board of Education.

1946 National Health Service Act

Following the publication in 1942 of the Beveridge Report the National Health Service in England and Wales was launched in 1948. It was intended to be free at the point of use, though prescription charges have since been introduced.

Aneurin (Nye) Bevan was the government minister who spearheaded the introduction of the NHS and a wider Welfare State.

1948 West Indian Immigrants

This was the year in which significant numbers of immigrants from the West Indies started to arrive. The most famous vessel that brought them was HMT Empire Windrush.

1951 Burgess and MacLean

Guy Burgess and Donald MacLean, two British Foreign Office officials, who were spying for the USSR, fled to Russia, followed by their associate Kim Philby.

The Mousetrap

The Mousetrap, by Agatha Christie, the world's longest running play (still running today) was first performed in London.

1952 First Jet Liner

The British De Havilland Comet was the first jet plane to enter passenger service.

Comet Airliner © John Braid / Shutterstock.com

Queen Elizabeth II ascends the throne

Queen Elizabeth II © Atlaspix / Shutterstock com

1953 Mount Everest Climbed

Mount Everest, 29,028ft high, was climbed by a British-led expedition under Sir John, later Lord, Hunt. The first two to reach the summit were Sir Edmund Hillary and Sherpa Tensing Norgay. Two British climbers, George Mallory and A. C. Irvine had gone missing in 1924, very near the top, but, to this day, nobody knows if they had actually reached it. Mallory's frozen body was found near the summit in 1999.

Mount Everest © Anton Rogozin / Shutterstock.com

Critchell Down Scandal

This estate in England, which had been compulsorily acquired by the State during the war, rather than being returned to its original owners, was going to be sold to the highest bidder. But after the resignation of a government minister and the suicide of one of the residents of the estate, it was decided that, thenceforth, full market value must be paid for all such property compulsorily purchased by the State.

1954 Four Minute Mile

Roger Banister broke this record at the Iffley Road running track in Oxford. His time was 3 minutes 59.4 seconds.

The Iffley Road Running Track, in Oxford, today

1956 Suez Crisis

The United Nations paid no attention to the valiant Hungarians, whose country had been invaded by Russia the day before, because they were concentrating their efforts on the Suez Canal where Britain and France had bombed Suez in their futile attempt to prevent Egypt nationalising and blocking off the Canal. Egypt had taken this course because, with the US dropping their plans to finance the Aswan Dam, the Egyptian Prime Minister, Gamal Abdul Nasser, sought to replace that finance with the revenues he would enjoy from nationalising the Suez Canal. Britain and France also hoped to thwart the Egyptians from resisting the Israelis who used this crisis as a cover for invading Sinai. Britain and France themselves were humiliated and Israel withdrew.

First video recorder was launched

1957 Jodrell Bank

This was the world's largest steerable radio telescope and was built in Cheshire.

Jodrell Bank © Asia Glab / Shutterstock.com

1958 The Common Market

The two Treaties of Rome, signed in 1957, established the European Economic Community (the European Common Market). Whilst known as the brainchild of Jean Monet, we now know that it was first proposed in occultist publications as early as 1914. The first signatories were Belgium, France, Italy, Luxemburg, the Netherlands and West Germany. The UK was not to join until 1973 and, in 2016, voted to leave what had then become a European Union.

The EU Parliament building in Brussels © Kiev.Victor / Shutterstock.com

First British Motorway

The first section of motorway to be built in Britain was the Preston By-pass (now part of the M6).

1962 DNA

In 1962, Francis Crick of the Cavendish Laboratory in Cambridge and James Watson of the USA were awarded the Nobel Prize for medicine for discovering the structure of DNA (Deoxyribonucleic Acid). (The first Nobel Prizes were awarded in 1901. They were founded by Alfred Nobel from the money he made from his invention of dynamite in 1875.)

1963 The Profumo affair

This scandal revealed that the Secretary of State for War, John Profumo, had slept with a showgirl named Christine Keeler who, in turn, had slept with a Russian spy. Profumo lied when subsequently questioned about it, which led to his resignation and also severely damaged the Macmillan government. Profumo devoted the rest of his life to charitable works in reparation.

1966 First Plaid Cymru MP elected to Westminster

1972 Bloody Sunday

The British army in Northern Ireland fired on a banned civil rights demonstration and killed 13 people. This triggered the violent troubles in Ulster and the imposition of Direct Rule by Westminster. The troubles began to ease only when the Good Friday agreement was signed in 1998.

1973 W. H. Auden dies

This British poet was born in 1907. With C. Day Lewis, Louis MacNeice and Stephen Spender, they formed a group of left wing poets in the 1930s; by the end of his life Auden turned away from Marxism and favoured Christianity.

1975 Death of P. G. Wodehouse

The comic writing of P. G. Wodehouse has led to him being described as the best writer of English in the twentieth century.

The re-created study of PG Wodehouse at Dulwich College, where he was at school. With kind permission of the Governors of Dulwich College©.

1976 Concorde enters service

This supersonic airliner, universally regarded for the beauty of its design, was withdrawn in 2003.

Concorde airliner © Dmitry Morgan / Shutterstock.com

National Exhibition Centre in Birmingham opens

Deaths of Agatha Christie and L. S. Lowry

Agatha Christie is to this day still world famous for her detective stories. She was born in 1890.

Lowry was a British painter who painted (mainly) bleak scenes with matchstick people. He was born in Manchester in 1887.

1978 Liverpool Anglican Cathedral completed

This is the biggest cathedral in Britain and was designed in Gothic style by Giles Gilbert Scott, himself a Catholic. He also designed the (now almost entirely replaced) red telephone boxes.

Left: Liverpool Cathedral © Mohamed Danon / Shutterstock.com. Right: The vast interior of Liverpool Anglican Cathedral with thanks to Andora Carver©.

1980 Mrs Thatcher and Ronald Reagan

In the 1980s, Margaret Thatcher, Prime Minister of the UK (1979-1990), and Ronald Reagan, President of the United States (1981-1989), formed a close alliance that was instrumental in bringing about the end of the Cold War and the collapse of Communism, including giving aid to such groups as the Solidarity movement (Solidarnosc) in Poland.

Ronald Reagan © Joseph Sohm. Margaret Thatcher © David Fowler. Both photos courtesy of Shutterstock. com

1982 Falklands War

Argentina invaded the Falkland Islands, and occupied other British territories, in the South Atlantic, but they were defeated and forced to withdraw by the British within 2 months. These islands were named after Viscount Falkland when Captain John Strong landed there in 1690. They had first brought Britain to the verge of war in 1771 and there had also been an international incident in 1848. In 1914, after the German victory at Coronel, all available allied warships were assembled in the South Atlantic and, at the Battle of the Falkland Isles, the German fleet that had won at Coronel was sunk with just one ship escaping.

Memorial to the Welsh Guards at Fitzroy on the Falkland Islands
© Jeremey Richards / Shutterstock.com

1984 Cabinet War Rooms

These underground and well-protected offices are where Churchill ran the British war effort during World War II. They were opened to the public this year.

The entrance to the (now called) Churchill War Rooms, with grateful thanks to © walklondon.com

1989 Internet, World Wide Web, Email and Text Messages

In November 1989 Tim Berners-Lee (later knighted) implemented the first successful Hypertext Transfer Protocol (HTTP) an event which is credited with launching the World Wide Web, or WWW. The WWW is a way of accessing information from the Internet, which is a global network consisting of millions of computers. The Internet started to be developed in the 1960s. The first email was sent in 1971 and the first text message in 1992.

1991 Gulf War

In 1990, Iraq, led by Saddam Hussein, invaded Kuwait. In 1991, British and American forces attacked Iraq (Operation Desert Storm) and successfully liberated Kuwait. At the same time, Hussein attacked the Kurds in Northern Iraq and forced 1 million to flee.

Maastricht Treaty

This treaty, building on the Single European Act of 1985, and introducing the plan for full European political union, was signed this year and later forced through the British Parliament amid great controversy. One reason for the controversy was because, amongst other things, this treaty ushered in European Regionalisation whereby the member countries would be (and now have been) divided up into European Regions with each Regional Assembly reporting not to national parliaments, but directly to Brussels. In due course this system of Regionalisation is set to see the closure of all European national governments, with just one seat of European national government at Brussels. Whilst this closure hasn't happened yet, the following are already organised or are about to be organised on a European regional basis:

- Fire
- Police
- Ambulance
- Voting in European elections
- Telephones
- Health services
- Planning

And it is likely that a great deal more will follow.

These assemblies were very unpopular in Britain, and were replaced by Regional Development Agencies in 2010.

1994 The Channel Tunnel opens

1997 Diana Princess of Wales killed in car crash in Paris

The memorial to the Princess of Wales in Paris

1998 The Scottish Parliament was re-established and opened in Edinburgh

1999 Welsh Assembly established in Cardiff

2003 Second Gulf War

The British and Americans overthrew the Iraqi regime run by Saddam Hussein in a short war. They maintained that he was a threat to world peace by holding an arsenal of "Weapons of Mass Destruction" (WMDs) and the West was determined to remove him.

Many suspected, and not without reason, that the real reason for the invasion was to secure Iraq's oil deposits for Western use. Of particular note was the failure by the invading forces to uncover any so-called WMDs, which had been the pretext for the invasion in the first place.

There was a further and related mystery, involving the apparent suicide in the summer of 2003 of Dr David Kelly, who had inspected the weapons held in Iraq and both knew and declared that Saddam Hussein had no weapons worthy of a US/British invasion. He is reported to have committed suicide shortly after revealing that the intelligence report on which the decision to go to war had been based, and which declared that Iraq possessed WMDs that were capable of delivery within 45 minutes, had been "sexed up." Many believe that the paucity of the evidence that he committed suicide suggests that he was actually murdered before he could undermine the British government's credibility any more.

Demonstrators demanding an inquest into the death of Dr David Kelly © Brian S / Shutterstock.com

In 2016 The Chilcot Report into the reasons for going into this war, and its aftermath, concluded that the government misjudged (overstated) the threat posed by Saddam Hussein (that it had not exhausted all peaceful options first) and that it also grossly underestimated the terrible consequences of its actions. Sir John Chilcot recommended that, in future, all aspects of any armed intervention should be "calculated, debated and challenged with the utmost rigour" before a final decision to go to war is made.

2005 London Bombings

On 7th July, over 50 people were killed by four bombs in London – an attack that appeared to copy the Madrid bombings of fifteen months earlier.

2006 Litvinenko's murder

Former Russian KGB employee, Alexander Litvinenko, who had fled to the West, was killed by nuclear (Polonium) poisoning in London. No-one could establish who had done it, but it had all the hallmarks of a KGB (now called FSB) killing. In 2015 it was announced by the US Security authorities that this was indeed the case.

2007 Treaty of Lisbon

This treaty, which had been called the European Constitution but had been rewritten and was now called the Treaty of Lisbon, was signed in 2007, ushering in a federal Europe and further emasculation of the powers of the individual European national governments. It had been rejected by the French and Dutch electorate, and was rejected the following year by Irish voters, but this did not stop the Brussels bureaucrats from proceeding with implementing the provisions of this self-amending treaty.

2009 Credit Crunch

While the recession caused by the Credit Crunch had begun in 2007, when banks started getting into serious financial difficulties for their profligate lending of money without asking sufficient questions, it was in this year that the severe effects of the resulting recession began to be noticed.

2013 Rise of UKIP

The UK Independence Party, founded in 1993, and which campaigned for the United Kingdom to withdraw from the European Union, gained 25% of the national vote in local elections. This party would win both the national elections to the EU Parliament and also two UK Parliamentary seats in by-elections the following year. (See also 2016 below.)

2014 The Scots reject independence (55% to 45%) in a referendum

2015 Queen Elizabeth II becomes Britain's longest serving monarch

2016 The UK votes (52% to 48%) to leave the European Union

The moment the result of the referendum was declared on television by the Electoral Commission – taken by the author during the BBC coverage. © BBC

The result of this referendum caused a political earthquake both in Britain and on the continent of Europe.

Appendices:

Appendices

1. British Kings and Queens:

Saxons and Danes

Name	Regnal Years	Religion	Ruled
Egbert	802 – 39	Catholic	Wessex
Ethelwulf	839 – 58	Catholic	Wessex
Ethelbald	858 – 60	Catholic	Wessex
Ethelbert	860 – 65	Catholic	Wessex
Ethelred	865 – 71	Catholic	Wessex
Alfred the Great	871 – 99	Catholic	Wessex
Edward the Elder	899 – 924	Catholic	Wessex but captured East Anglia and Mercia

English Monarchs

Athelstan the Glorious	924 – 39	Catholic	First King of All England
Edmund	939 – 46	Catholic	England
Edred	946 – 55	Catholic	England
Edwy the Fair (Edwig)	955 – 59	Catholic	England
Edgar the Peaceful	959 – 75	Catholic	England
Edward the Martyr	975 – 78	Catholic	England
Ethelred II (The Unready)	978 – 1016	Catholic	England
Edmund Ironside	1016	Catholic	England
Canute	1016 – 35	Catholic	England, Denmark, Norway and parts of Sweden
Harold I (Harefoot)	1035 – 40	Catholic	England
Hardecanute	1040 – 42	Catholic	England and Denmark
St Edward The Confessor	1042 – 66	Catholic	England
Harold II (Godwinson)	1066	Catholic	England

Norman Conquest 1066

Norman	Regnal Years	Religion	Queen / Consort
William I (The Conqueror)	1066 – 87	Catholic	Matilda of Flanders
William II (Rufus)	1087 – 1100	Catholic	Not Married
Henry I (Beauclerc)	1100 – 35	Catholic	Matilda of Scotland
Stephen	1135 – 54	Catholic	Matilda of Boulogne

Plantagenet	Regnal Years	Religion	Queen / Consort
Henry II	1154 – 89	Catholic	Eleanor of Aquitaine
Richard I (Lionheart)	1189 – 99	Catholic	Berengaria of Navarre
John	1199 – 1216	Catholic	1. Isabel of Gloucester (div) 2. Isabella of Angouleme
Henry III	1216 – 1272	Catholic	Eleanor of Provence
Edward I (Longshanks and Hammer of the Scots)	1272 – 1307	Catholic	Eleanor of Castille
Edward II	1307 – 27	Catholic	Isabella of France
Edward III	1327 – 77	Catholic	Philippa of Hainault
Richard II	1377 – 99	Catholic	1. Anne of Bohemia (died) 2. Isabella of France
Lancaster			
Henry IV (Bolingbroke)	1399 – 1413	Catholic	1. Mary de Bohun. 2. Johanna of Navarre
Henry V	1413 – 22	Catholic	Catherine of Valois
Henry VI	1422 – 61, 1470 – 71	Catholic	Margaret of Anjou
York			
Edward IV	1461 – 70, 1471 – 83	Catholic	Elizabeth Woodville
Edward V	1483	Catholic	Not married
Richard III	1483 – 85	Catholic	Anne Neville
Tudor			
Henry VII	1485 – 1509	Catholic	Elizabeth of York
Henry VIII	1509 – 47	Schismatic	1. Catherine of Aragon. 2. Anne Boleyn 3. Jane Seymour 4. Anne of Cleeves. 5. Catherine Howard. 6. Catherine Parr
Edward VI	1547 – 53	Protestant	Not married
Mary	1553 – 58	Catholic	King Philip II of Spain
Elizabeth I	1558 – 1603	Protestant	Not married

British Monarchs

Stuart			
James I (VI of Scotland)	1603 – 25	Protestant	Anne of Denmark
Charles I	1625 – 49	Protestant	Henrietta Maria
Commonwealth	*1653 – 59*	Protestant	

	Regnal Years	Religion	Queen / Consort
Charles II	1660 – 85	Catholic	Catherine of Portugal
James II	1685 – 88 He died in France in 1701	Catholic	1. Anne Hyde 2. Mary of Modena
William III & Mary II, (Mary died 1694)	1688 – 1702	Protestant	Joint Monarchy
Anne	1702 – 14	Protestant	George of Denmark
Hanover			
George I	1714 – 27	Protestant	Sophia Dorothea
George II	1727 – 60	Protestant	Caroline of Brandenburg-Ansbach
George III	1760 – 1820	Protestant	Charlotte of Mecklenburg-Strelitz
George IV	1820 – 30	Protestant	1. Mrs Fitzherbert. 2. Caroline of Brunswick.
William IV	1830 – 37	Protestant	Adelaide
Victoria	1837 – 1901	Protestant	Prince Albert of Saxe-Coburg Gotha
Saxe-Coburg Gotha			
Edward VII	1901 – 10	Protestant	Alexandra of Denmark
Windsor (Changed from Saxe-Coburg Gotha 1917)			
George V	1910 – 36	Protestant	Princess Mary of Teck
Edward VIII	1936 (Abdicated before Coronation)	Protestant	Wallis Simpson
George VI	1936 – 52	Protestant	Elizabeth Bowes-Lyon
Elizabeth II	1952 –	Protestant	Prince Philip, Duke of Edinburgh

Willie, Willie
A rhyme to help you remember the order in which British Kings and Queens have reigned:

Willie, Willie, Harry, Stee
Harry, Dick, John, Harry Three,
One Two Three Neds, Richard Two,
Henry Four, Five, Six, then who?
Edward Four, Five, Dick the bad,
Harry's twain and Ned the lad,
Mary Bessie, James the vain,
Charlie, Charlie, James again.
Will and Mary, Anna Gloria,
Four Georges, William and Victoria.
Edward Seven and Georgie Five,
Edward, George and Liz alive.

And to help you remember the royal houses:

No Plan Like Yours To Study History Wisely.

Viz:
Norman
Plantagenet
Lancaster
York
Tudor
Stuart
Hanover
Windsor

2. British Prime Ministers

Con = Conservative, Lib = Liberal, Lab = Labour, Coal = Coalition

Robert Walpole	Whig	1721 – 42
Spencer Compton	Whig	1742 – 3
Henry Pelham	Whig	1743 – 54
Thomas Pelham	Whig	1754 – 6
William Cavendish	Whig	1756 – 7
Thomas Pelham	Whig	1757 – 62
John Stuart	Tory	1762 – 3
George Grenville	Whig	1763 – 5
Charles Watson Wentworth	Whig	1765 – 6
William Pitt (the Elder)	Whig	1766 – 7
Augustus Henry Fitzroy	Whig	1767 – 70
Lord North	Tory	1770 – 82
Charles Watson Wentworth	Whig	1782
William Petty	Whig	1782 – 3
William Henry Cavendish	Coal	1783
William Pitt (the Younger)	Tory	1783 – 1801
Henry Addington	Tory	1801 – 4
William Pitt (the Younger)	Tory	1804 – 6
William Wyndham Grenville	Whig	1806 – 7
William Henry Cavendish	Coal	1807 – 9
Spencer Percival	Tory	1809 – 12
Robert Banks Jenkinson	Tory	1812 – 27
George Canning	Tory	1827
Frederick John Robinson	Tory	1827 – 8
The Duke of Wellington	Tory	1828 – 30
Charles Grey	Whig	1830 – 4
Viscount Melbourne	Whig	1834
Robert Peel	Con	1834 – 5
William Lamb	Whig	1835 – 41
Robert Peel	Con	1841 – 6
Lord John Russell	Lib	1846 – 52
The Earl of Derby	Con	1852
George Hamilton Gordon	Peelite	1852 – 5
Henry John Temple	Lib	1855 – 8
The Earl of Derby	Con	1858 – 9
Viscount Palmerston	Lib	1859 – 65
Lord John Russell	Lib	1865 – 6
The Earl of Derby	Con	1866 – 8
Benjamin Disraeli	Con	1868
William Ewart Gladstone	Lib	1868 – 74
Benjamin Disraeli	Con	1874 – 80
William Ewart Gladstone	Lib	1880 – 5
Marquis of Salisbury	Con	1885 – 6
William Ewart Gladstone	Lib	1886
Marquis of Salisbury	Con	1886 – 92
William Ewart Gladstone	Lib	1892 – 4

Earl of Rosebery	Lib	1894 – 5
Marquis of Salisbury	Con	1895 – 1902
Arthur James Balfour	Con	1902 – 5
Henry Campbell-Bannerman	Lib	1905 – 8
Herbert Henry Asquith	Lib & Coal	1908 – 1916
David Lloyd George	Coal	1916 – 22
Andrew Bonar Law	Con	1922 – 3
Stanley Baldwin	Con	1923 – 4
James Ramsey MacDonald	Lab	1924
Stanley Baldwin	Con	1924 – 29
James Ramsey MacDonald	Lab	1929 – 31
James Ramsey Macdonald	National Gov	1931 – 5
Stanley Baldwin	National Gov	1935 – 7
Arthur Neville Chamberlain	National Gov	1937 – 40
Winston Leonard Spencer Churchill	Coal	1940 – 5
Clement Richard Attlee	Lab	1945 – 51
Winston Leonard Spencer Churchill	Con	1951 – 5
Robert Anthony Eden	Con	1955 – 7
Maurice Harold Macmillan	Con	1957 – 63
Alec Frederick Douglas-Home	Con	1963 – 4
James Harold Wilson	Lab	1964 – 70
Edward Richard George Heath	Con	1970 – 74
James Harold Wilson	Lab	1974 – 6
Leonard James Callaghan	Lab	1976 – 9
Margaret Hilda Thatcher	Con	1979 – 90
John Major	Con	1990 – 7
Anthony Charles Lynton Blair	Lab	1997 – 2007
James Gordon Brown	Lab	2007 – 2010
David William Donald Cameron	Con/Lib Coal	2010 – 2015
David William Donald Cameron	Con	2015 – 2016
Theresa Mary May	Con	2016 –

3. Scottish Kings and Queens

Malcolm II	1005 – 34
Duncan I	1034 – 40
Macbeth	1040 – 57
Lulach	1057 – 58
Malcolm III	1058 – 93
Donald III (Donald Bane)	1093 – 4
Duncan II	1094
Donald III (Donald Bane)	1094 – 7
Edgar	1097 – 1107
Alexander I	1107 – 24
David I	1124 – 53
Malcolm IV (the Maiden)	1153 – 65
William I (the Lion)	1165 – 1214
Alexander II	1214 – 49
Alexander III	1249 – 86
Margaret (Maid of Norway)	1286 – 90
Interregnum	1290 – 2
John Balliol	1292 – 6
Interregnum	1296 – 1306
Robert the Bruce	1306 – 29
David II	1329 – 71
Robert II	1371 – 90
Robert III	1390 – 1406
James I	1406 – 37
James II	1437 – 60
James III	1460 – 88
James IV	1488 – 1513
James V	1513 – 42
Mary Queen of Scots	1542 – 67
James VI	1567 – 1625

(Scottish and English Kingdoms thereafter united)

17. Family Trees

Appendix 4a

Family Tree to show how the last pre-Norman kings were related

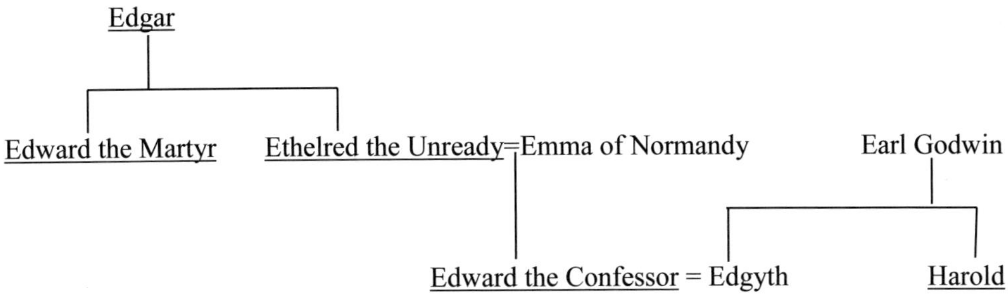

William the Conqueror was the grand-nephew of Emma of Normandy

Appendix 4b

Family Tree to show how John of Gaunt was related to the kings of England between Edward III and Henry VI

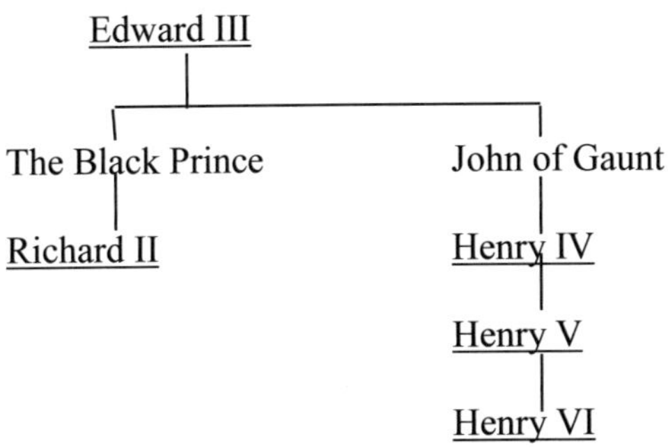

Appendix 4c

Family Tree to show how the Tudor Monarchs were related

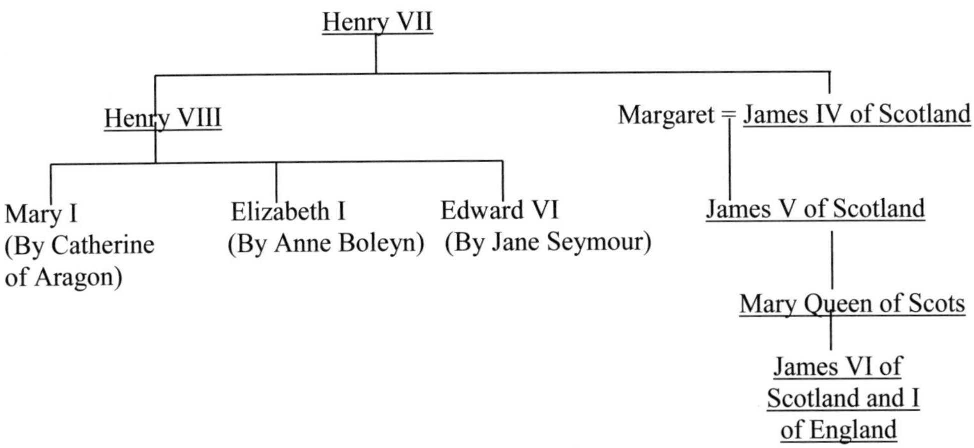

In all of the above family trees, underlined = Monarchs

Appendix 4d
Family Tree to show how the key figures involved in the Wars of the Roses were related

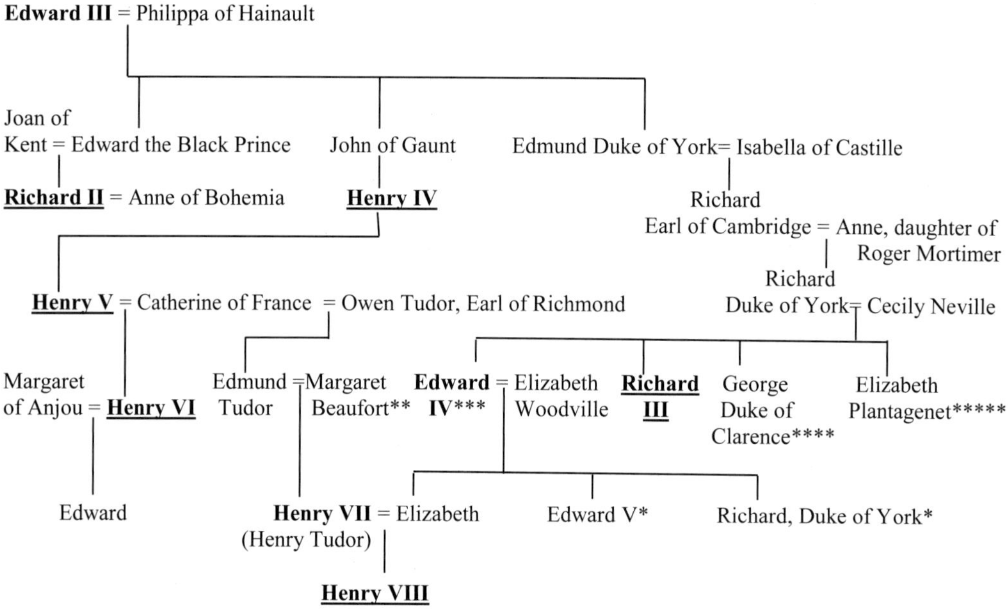

*= The Two Little Princes.

** Margaret Beaufort was the great granddaughter of John of Gaunt.

***Recent research (2012) seems to, not merely suggest but, prove that Edward IV was illegitimate since his father was away fighting when he was conceived. Thus it appears that both Edward IV was illegitimate but so too would have been his children, Elizabeth, Edward V and Richard Duke of York. In fact the children were illegitimate on two counts – first their father was illegitimate and second, their father had been secretly married before he married Elizabeth Woodville. These two factors would have given Richard III even greater claim to the throne.

**** George, Duke of Clarence was drowned in a butt of Malmsey wine on the orders of Edward IV for declaring that he, Edward, was illegitimate, which we now know was true.

*****With all the claimants to the throne either dead or illegitimate, the rightful heirs to the throne should have descended from Elizabeth Plantagenet. However a recent rightful heir, Michael Abney-Hastings, who died in Australia in 2012, was not interested in making a claim.

Kings of England shown in bold.

Kings whose names are underlined have had one, or more, plays written about their lives by William Shakespeare.

British History Index

Please note that, in this index, no page numbers are given. Instead each topic is given a reference date, which means that one will find the topic required under the relevant date shown in the Reference Date column ↓

Index

Please remember the note at the top of page 233

Please remember the note at the top of page 233

Index

Please remember the note at the top of page 233

Index

Please remember the note at the top of page 233

Index

Please remember the note at the top of page 233

Index

Please remember the note at the top of page 233

Index

Please remember the note at the top of page 233

Please remember the note at the top of page 233

Index

Please remember the note at the top of page 233

Index

Please remember the note at the top of page 233

Index

Please remember the note at the top of page 233

Index

Please remember the note at the top of page 233

Index

Please remember the note at the top of page 233

Index

Please remember the note at the top of page 233

Index

Please remember the note at the top of page 233

Please remember the note at the top of page 233

Index

Please remember the note at the top of page 233

Index

Please remember the note at the top of page 233

Index

Please remember the note at the top of page 233

Order Form
British History – An Illustrated Guide

Retail Price in UK by post £18 per copy (£15 + £3 postage and packing.)

For bulk orders, orders by educational establishments or orders from outside the UK, email info@stedwardspress.co.uk

Our no-quibble guarantee is that if you are not happy with your purchase, you can return the order to us with proof of payment and receive a full refund.

Your order
Please send me ____ copies of *British History – An Illustrated Guide* (please allow 28 days for delivery)

Your details
Full name ______________________________

Address ____

____

PostCode________Telephone____________Email__________________________

Payment
I enclose a cheque for £_______________ OR Please charge my credit card
(Orders through credit cards from overseas will be taken in Sterling and converted by your credit company into your currency of origin)

Name as it appears on card ______________________________________

Type of card (whether it's Visa, MasterCard etc) ____________________

Card number____

Expiry date ___ /___ Last three digits of the number on the back of card _______
(The last 2 lines above will be cut off and destroyed once payment has been processed.)

Signature ____ Date _____________

Placing your order
1. Print or copy this form and fill it in. Please be sure to fill in all relevant sections.
2. Send your order to: Or scan and Email to info@stedwardspress.co.uk

St Edwards Press Ltd
C/o Hugh Williams
20 Barra Close
Highworth, Wilts, SN6 7HX
United Kingdom
(Phone 01793 762417 (mobile 07812 426538) – or leave message at 01752 334950)

Please note that since this business is run from home, it is possible that the telephone may not always be answered. Please accept our apologies if this happens to you.

How this book came to be written - A word by the author.

There seem to be a number of different types of history reference book and, to me, many of them suffer from certain failings: Either they consist of page after page of verbiage, with few paragraphs, even fewer headings and small type face. (I have to say that I wonder how anyone can find any facts quickly from a book that is designed like that);

Or the contents are arranged alphabetically, which, I think, is a distinct disadvantage when it comes to history, because I think one needs things in *chronological* order;

Or they are written for children and have so much happening on each page (words and illustrations all over the place) that I think they confuse rather than enlighten;

Or they dumb down the whole subject of history, the very thought, and look, of which I find thoroughly off-putting.

And then there is another problem with many history books in that the illustrations tend to be all bundled together in a few pages in the middle of the book, miles away from the text to which they relate.

In short, I have found most history reference books to be not very helpful.

I read once that Bamber Gascoigne wrote his wonderful *Encyclopaedia of Britain* because, he said, "I needed it on my shelves" - a course of action that I can well understand. In other words, if a book that one wants to read doesn't exist, then one probably needs to write it oneself. So I have decided to follow his example, gather up what I have learned about this subject and write my own guide to British History. This is the result and I would be interested to know what readers think.

Hugh Williams 2016 (info@stedwardspress.co.uk)

Space for Notes

Step 1 Before the Coming of the Romans – 4000BC to 55BC

Space for Notes

Step 2 From the Romans to the Norman Invasion – 55BC to 1066

Space for Notes

Step 3 Norman History – 1066 to 1154

Space for Notes

Step 4 Plantagenet History – 1154 to 1399

Space for Notes

Step 5 The Houses of Lancaster and York – 1399 to 1485

Space for Notes

Step 6 Tudor History – 1485 to 1603

Space for Notes

Step 7 Stuart History – 1603 to 1714

Space for Notes

Step 8 Hanoverian History – 1714 to 1901

Space for Notes

Step 9 The House of Windsor – 1901 to the present day